Route 66 Cycle Challenge
Kevee's Story

by

Kevin Lynch

Grosvenor House
Publishing Limited

The right of Kevin Lynch to be identified as the author of this
work has been asserted by him in accordance with Section 78
of the Copyright, Designs and Patents Act 1988

The book cover picture is copyright to Kevin Lynch

This book is published by
Grosvenor House Publishing Ltd
28-30 High Street, Guildford, Surrey, GU1 3EL.
www.grosvenorhousepublishing.co.uk

A CIP record for this book
is available from the British Library

ISBN 978-1-78148-692-4

For Sandra

Always by my side no matter what I do,
without you who knows where I would be.

There are so many people I need to thank, please forgive me if I miss anyone out.

Becky, always with me in my heart and constantly spreading the word about our challenge, a prouder father I could not be.

My Mother who has never stopped believing in me from the day I was born.

My Father and sisters for their continual encouragement.

Gill and Mick for the love and support you have always shown me.

The riders who came and went, your contribution was immeasurable I thank you all.

Friends and family who donated online or came to one of our events.

Verulamians Rugby Club and The Crooked Billet.

Our sponsors and kind friends who donated raffle and auction prizes.

My L2P and three Cities buddies, you have been inspirational to me since the day I met you all, so many nice people doing so many good things.

My friends at work for listening to me rant on, day after day, especially Matt for his calming advice.

Casey, you pulled me round and kept me focused, thank you son.

The crew, what can I say, your hard work made it happen, you kept us going in difficult situations. Steve, thanks for letting me use some of the 700 photos in this book, they tell the story on their own.

My fellow riders, I don't think we can ever truly explain to anyone what we went through in those seven days, but we made it in one piece.

Ross, what can I say? This really was the trip of a lifetime and I thank you for being my friend.

Bernice the work you and Sandra put into the ball and all our events was second to none.

Daniel Bradbury for all his work on the cover design.

Contents

Foreword

Route 66 Cycle Challenge, what's that all about?

The trip was conceived some two years prior to the actual challenge starting, this is my story told from my perspective, of how the trip unravelled. Many riders joined and left, the financial burden just being too great, others just didn't seem to gel with the team. The final eight of us who saw the fundraising through and eventually rode the route became like brothers. The thing with brothers is they often have different opinions of what should be happening; who should be doing what and when. I have trawled through emails and Facebook comments that have been sent and posted over the past two years to refresh my memory to keep this as honest as it can be.

To my fellow teammates, I love you all, I have written this book as I saw events unfold. I hope you enjoy reading it and it takes you back to all the good and not so good moments. To anyone reading this thinking of embarking on their own personnel challenge I say, if you really want it you can do it, just be prepared to work very hard for it. This was the hardest thing I have ever done in my life, at times terrifying and that was not just the toilet on the RV.

Many people have gone before us and completed much greater challenges, many have raised far greater amounts of money, to us this was our challenge of a lifetime, eight average Joe's pushing themselves to physical and mental extremes.

Who would crack first? Who didn't train enough? Who overdid it before the start? All these questions will be answered but most importantly did we take enough chamois and sudocrem? Ouch!!!!

I hope you enjoy reading this book as much as I enjoyed writing it and honestly if someone like me can complete a challenge like this, the world really is your oyster.

Kevee

The Route 66 Team

Riders:

Ross
Mark
Casey
Andy
Mick
Danny
Barry or Bazza
Kevee

The Crew:

Greg
Will
James
Steve
Ian
King Kenny

Support Crew:

Sandra and Bernice

Riders we lost along the way:

Billy
Roy
Big Dan
Greg W
Hyphen
Sam
Neil
Gez

Skyline/Logistics:

Sally

Chapter 1

And So To Chicago

Andy and Mick had headed off a day earlier on a BA flight, the rest of the riders opted for the Virgin flight, as they let you take 23kg of sports equipment free of charge. The old bike bags were packed to the brim with anything we couldn't fit in the suitcase. Ross's bike bag was huge weighing more than his bike, it was going to be touch and go whether or not it would fit through the door of the plane.

Mark was meeting us at the airport whilst the rest of us met up in Welham Green, including Sandra, my wife and Bernice, Ross's wife, who were intending to drive Route 66 Thelma and Louise style. My daughter Bex dropped us off and it was quite emotional as my son was riding with us and Sandra was shadowing us all the way. Bex had to work, so my family wasn't going to be together which seemed very strange to me. Bex had written Casey and I a card each, which Sandra gave to us once we were on route I have to say I had a tear in my eye, she would be with us in spirit, of that we could be sure.

Ross and Bernice own a bus company and laid on a London Routemaster bus to transport us to the Airport. Within 10 minutes of starting the journey Bernice had the bottles of Prosecco opened and we all enjoyed a glass at 5am in the morning, a tad early for me and certainly for Sandra who seemed to evade the bottle very cleverly.

This was it, we were finally going to do it, or attempt to do it. I looked around at the others, was this fine bunch of fellows ready for the challenge ahead? I thought yes but took another swig of the bubbly stuff just to reassure myself.

Barry or Big Bazza or Rapha Bal as he likes to be called had a nice presentation pack ready to show to the Virgin check-in girls explaining what we were about, he tried to blag an upgrade and managed to get extra leg room seats. If you stand at about eight foot four, as he and Casey do, it certainly was a relief for those guys. Bernice had sorted herself and Ross out, they had some sort of reward points and were travelling upper class. Mark arrived and he was going premium economy, this left Bazza, Oh Danny Boy, Casey, Sandra and myself in economy. It was the builders section of the team having all worked in the trade at some time. Technically Casey had finished his degree, (not in building) but as he wasn't looking for a job until after the challenge and was working for me, so he is classed as a builder, he has been working for me since he was about five.

The flight was great, we were all very excited, the crew were very interested in what we were doing and put out an announcement telling the rest of the passengers.

Ross had been dealing with Skyline, our logistics partners and there had been a few emails asking who was arriving on what day. It was my understanding from earlier meetings that the rooms were booked for one night only and any earlier arrivals were up to us to sort out. It had got a bit confusing and some of the team were expecting to be picked up at the airport. When we arrived a text came through from Mick explaining a major cock-up on taxis and accommodation.

It was one of those things really, in all the excitement leading up to departure, we hadn't really looked at the detail. It wasn't going to dampen our spirit, nothing could at this time, looking back it would have been nice to all travel out together, start as a team finish as a team.

The hotel was basic but clean, the staff on the front desk treated us like long lost friends, Mick and Andy having already told them what we were about to undertake. I think they thought we were mad cycling from Chicago to LA, which was some two and a half thousand miles away. They had never heard of people doing this before, unless it was in a car or on a motorbike. They were under the impression we were super fit cyclists, how wrong could they be? The hotel was way out of town, so we choose to stay nearby for our first night. We checked in and headed across to a local bar that also served food. It was a bit rough around the edges, loud rock music playing with bikers on one side of the bar and police enjoying a meal on the other side. Mick and Andy joined us along with two of the crew Greg, the tour leader, and Kenny, the tour granddad, as he would later be known.

We sunk a few beers and ate well, the bill came to $20 each, either they can't add up in Chicago or this was my sort of pub.

I headed back with Ross, Sandra, Bernice, Andy and Mick, leaving some of the others to carry on drinking, Mark and Casey who were rooming together staying out the latest only leaving when one of the clientele got tasered by the local police.

The next day we headed into town to do the tourist bit and to checkout the start. We left the crew to go pick up the RV's and collect the rest of the crew from the airport. It was a bit of a trek in, I think about forty minutes on the train. We all posed beside the start sign for a photo, you could feel the atmosphere; it was mixed with excitement but also apprehension. We grabbed a coffee and I wandered back out to the start sign on my own. I sparked up a cigar, a bad habit of mine, and remember looking at the sign and thinking to myself shit this is real. Tomorrow there would be no turning back, Christ had I trained enough? Probably not. I had spoken with Casey on many occasions about this trip, it's safe to say out of all the guys, we had cycled a lot less than anyone else, but we had put in a tremendous amount of gym work. Casey had been lecturing me for months on what classes I needed to attend and what I should and should not be eating. I thought I was the dad!

The only advice I had been giving him was, under no circumstance must we let the team down, we never give in no matter what happens. Maybe I draw on this from playing rugby; you rely on your teammates as much as they rely on you. If you are 60–nil down at half-time (which I have been on many occasions) you keep going, don't let the bastards nil you, even if you are battered beyond belief you don't show it: "Once a Vee (Verulamians Rugby Club) always a Vee." I'll take that spirit onto Route 66. Yes I was pumped up now; I started to head back to the others, no wait a mo maybe another cigar, that's the spirit. We walked around Chicago for a few hours, it rained and we all got a bit wet, not great preparation but I don't think anyone really cared.

We split up on the way back, Ross, Casey, Bernice, Sandra and I headed to pick up the car for Sandra and Bernice's epic road trip. We had booked a car already but upgraded it to the biggest four by four they had, we knew the luggage space would come in handy and if we encountered any rough roads they could be sure this beast would get through. The space on the RV's would be limited so we had decided to leave our bike bags and main suitcases with the girls. This proved to be a great plan, as when we reached Santa Monica we still had fresh smelling clothes for our onward journey.

Upon our return to the hotel, our homes for the next week had arrived. They looked like something out of a seventies TV series I'm sure the Brady Bunch would have loved them. You can't judge a book by the cover, or so I'm told so I climbed on board, they were basic but roomy, not quite like the Sky Pro Cycling team bus I was hoping for but fit for purpose. We set about putting caution stickers and sponsor logos that Ross had made on the RV's, it was all looking very professional.

We showered and headed back to the local for our last meal before the start tomorrow, vowing not to drink in preparation for the early start. The rest of the crew were starting to arrive and a very experienced team we had too. Will, Ian and James, I had encountered on previous trips and Steve seemed like a nice chap.

We ordered food plus a beer, well one might help me sleep I may have had another. We discussed Greg's plan of 40 mile stints I was seriously worrying about this because I had trained for 30 mile or two hour stints whatever came first. They explained the 40 mile logic. Two riders would go in the front bus also known as the sleeper and travel 120 miles, Skyline marking the route with the famous orange arrows. Four riders would get in the back bus; two would start on the road and complete 40 miles. The next two riders would cycle from 40 to 80 then the next two from 80 to 120. When we reached the front bus the riders just completing would jump in and get their rest as the bus moved on another 120 miles. The riders who had been in the front bus would have jumped out to do the 120 to 160 stint.

I headed back to the hotel room with Sandra, I slept surprisingly well, it must have been the two beers. I woke early as I always do and wandered downstairs, I grabbed a coffee and sat on a bench outside, I smoked a couple of cigars. It was starting to really dawn on me that there was no turning back, this was it. I had trained well, but should I have done more? Fourteen guys together for a week, how would I handle that? I shouldn't be worrying at this stage, it was time to embrace the challenge, the mother road was waiting and we would soon be upon her. Other people started to appear all looking a bit anxious but excited, so it wasn't just me, we were all in the same boat from the riders to the crew to Sandra and Bernice, it was time, we loaded up and headed to the start.

Chapter 2

From The Beginning
And London To Paris

People are always asking me how I got into cycling; I'm not that sure I am into it. I have always liked watching the Olympic track cycling and Sean Kelly in the tours from years gone by. I don't cycle a lot really, I just seem to take on a challenge now and again.

I remember Sandra and I being away with Ross and Bernice about three and half years ago in Cyprus. We were all sitting around the pool when I pulled my Tour De France guidebook out to have a read, the ridicule I got from Ross and Bernice, they were laughing and couldn't believe what I was reading. Sandra explained I loved watching it and would sit all day watching it if I could. They didn't understand, how boring was that? Every time I got it out during the holiday the same abuse ensued.

A while after we got back we were talking about riding London to Paris. How that came about I'll never know, we didn't even have bikes, not proper road bikes and I wasn't going to ride my mountain bike 300 miles.

Before I knew it we had signed up for London to Paris, May 2011.

I started to read up on bikes, I set myself a budget of £600, which seemed a lot of money to me, but if I was going to ride three hundred miles I wanted to be comfortable.

Ross got his bike first, an all-singing, all-dancing carbon road bike I'm thinking he's got a head start, so I shopped around and purchased my Planet X, as it seemed to give you a lot of kit for your money. I must admit my £600 budget went straight out of the window, my bike arrived around Christmas but the weather was so bad I couldn't get out on it. I then managed to fall from a ladder, only a couple of steps but my coccyx wasn't very happy with the pole I landed on. So my training was going none too well. We attended a meet and information day in London for our forthcoming cycle to Paris, this is where we first met Mick and Andy whom we had been chatting to on the L2P May 2011 Facebook page. We got on really well from the off, Billy was also there, who would later join the Route 66 team, but subsequently withdraw. We also met Donna and Sue who would also end up great mates.

So my training prior to the trip was about 100 odd miles the longest being 40 miles, not great preparation.

The trip itself was fantastic, we set off riding alongside Billy and his mate Roy, I thought I was doing ok for the first hour or so. Knowing we were taking the ferry from Dover and our luggage was meeting us in France I had a great idea to take a pair of flip flops, so when we were on the ferry I could walk around easily rather than struggle in my cleats. As we cycled along someone shouted that I had dropped my flip-flops so I stopped to retrieve them, Ross carried on with Billy and Roy and no matter how hard I tried a couldn't catch them. I settled into a rhythm, my mind was playing tricks on me, was this going to be a solo trip to Paris? I had to just get on with it. I was approaching the water stop, maybe they had waited for me. I was in luck Ross was there, he said he had been waiting for twenty minutes and wanted to get off, I needed a rest so told him to go if he wanted too. I didn't want to hold him up, that first hour proved to be the only time we cycled together on the four day trip. Lucky for me Andy and Mick were at the water stop and had seen I was on my own. I teamed up with them and we had a slower ride stopping off at cafés and bars. I met so many people on this trip that have remained good friends, big Dan was a fantastic guy who was part of the original Route 66 team and Jacqui and Nathan who joined us on the three cities ride, but the whole 100 odd people were fantastic and I think that's what gave me such a buzz. I would like to name you all but it would be a long list.

Sally was our tour leader on the trip, it was a Skyline event and I must say we were mighty impressed. The whole thing ran like clockwork from day one until completion, the only thing the riders had to worry about was riding, everything else was sorted. I could get used to this sort of trip the only thing that wasn't right was my saddle or was it my backside? I'm not sure which but they didn't seem to be getting on very well. As we cycled across the French countryside I got to know

Mick and Andy and they became friends who I felt I had known for ages. Andy would love to sit on the front with Mick in behind him and I would take the rear. If the roads were quiet we would cycle three abreast and chat. Every now and then we would stop to help people out with punctures or just cycle along with other people. As the days went on I became stronger and the last day I was really into my riding and was pulling the others along. It was a joint effort the whole four days; the last day of stopping off for a beer here and there was a fitting end. We arrived last at the holding point outside Paris but it wasn't a race.

I look back in great fondness on that trip it was the start of things to come. My life style would change over the next two and a half years, albeit for the better.

What do you do after that? I was looking into doing a coast-to-coast ride across America, It seemed to take over a month and it would be a long time off work, so it was a non-starter really. Ross then came up with Route 66 in a week. He contacted us, Mick was straight in as was Billy and Roy. I thought about it for a while, I didn't want to miss out but could I afford it, could it be done? Andy was quiet but that might have been because he didn't check his Facebook daily. I calculated it would take four teams of two riding fifteen mph per session to achieve this in a week, I would be well off that pace I'm more of a plodder. I spoke to Ross he was going to approach Skyline to see if they would be interested in running it for us, as they run thousands of charity events such as London to Paris and are very well organised.

So Ross, Mick, Andy, Billy, Roy and myself were in.

Skyline were interested which was fantastic news; if we didn't have to sort all the logistics out it would be so much more fun.

We had a meeting up in London the guys were really excited, Ross and Mick were setting a target of raising £100,000 for charity. We talked about getting celebrities involved, the BBC and Children in Need or Comic Relief. We also discussed getting corporate sponsorship to help pay for the trip. We thought we could make it a world record attempt, had anyone ridden it in a week before?

There was a lot of enthusiasm Mick and Ross were driving things along with constant emails and Facebook posts. The next thing was to go and meet Skyline, Ross went along. He met up with Sally who had been team leader on our London to Paris ride. It wasn't something they had done before but they were enthusiastic. They would look into it to see if it could be achieved and work out some sort of costing. The guys were all confident in obtaining corporate sponsorship but I was a bit sceptical. The country was in the middle of a recession and major companies were having to tighten their belts. You looked around on Facebook and Twitter and it seemed everyone and his dog was taking part in a charity fundraiser. Would we be able to cover the tour cost and would we raise any money for charity? It was a question that would linger on and on.

We needed another two teammates so it was decided we would invite big Dan Bradbury a guy who I had got on very well with when we met him on L2P. Dan was well up for it and asked if his mate Greg W could join us, as it would help him to have a training partner who lived nearby where he lived in Norfolk. Greg W had also been on L2P although none of us could remember him. It was agreed and the first incarnation of the eight-man team was born (little did we know that this line up would change and change on many occasions).

There was a big L2P reunion night coming up in London we thought we could meet up a couple of hours earlier to talk about Route 66. We hadn't told anyone yet about what we were planning so we agreed we would announce it later that night.

It was great to see the others from L2P, Jacqui who had cycled most of the trip on one knee after a fall early on. Donna and Sue who enjoyed a laugh and a drink. Colette who had cycled a stretch with us, Andres, he was a lovely chap and Hyphen. Judging by the interest from our friends I started thinking we were at the start of something major if we could see it through.

We were still unsure if we should go with eight or ten riders. With ten it would give us a good chance even if we lost riders through injury. Hyphen was chasing Ross to be added to the team, Ross put it two the rest of us, a couple of the guys were not keen so it was deemed best to stick with eight to save upsetting anyone.

The next big step was selecting a charity, with eight opinions it could prove a little tricky. Mick and Andy were keen to go with Help for Heroes and arranged a meeting.

Roy, Ross, Andy, Mick and I attended. What can I say we came away all of us thinking this was the charity.

We had contacted a few other charities but didn't get much response apart from The Willow Foundation. Myself, Mick, Dan and Roy went along to a meeting. We met Carol for the first time and she told us the story of the charity, how Bob Wilson and his wife Megs had set it up in memory of their daughter Anna who sadly lost her battle against cancer. Willow was Anna's nickname; she had loved the special days spent with her family leading up to her passing away. Bob and Megs wanted to give other people the chance to have special days with family and as a family man myself this really struck home with me, as it did with the other guys.

We all had to make a choice, one of the guys probably wouldn't take part if we did it for Help for Heroes, but we were all a bit undecided so we thought let's do it for both and this seemed to sort everything out and we were all happy.

We had loads of things to sort out – the name of the challenge – that needed to be right, a logo we handed that over to big Dan. Mick and Ross were still full on trying to get people geed up. Roy and Billy were a bit quiet, as was Andy. I was excited but had a lot happening at work and still didn't feel I was putting 100% in yet. I'd played rugby a few weeks earlier and had sprained my ankle quite badly, things were not going well. I needed to make a decision, was I going to be able to afford it? I knew the lads were confident in getting sponsorship but I really wasn't. My rugby career was at an end, not that it was an illustrious career but I had enjoyed playing. Could I raise the sponsorship money Mick wanted us to raise? Needless to say a lot was going through my mind. I think at this point I sat down and discussed it all with Sandra. She was very supportive and told me to see it through, knowing me better than anyone she knows I need a focus. Work is very important that's how you get money to do things but most blokes need something other than work, whether it's going to watch football, fishing or going to the pub, guys do need an outlet.

I decided to throw myself into the challenge and do everything I could possibly do to make it work. We had another meeting coming up with Sally at Skyline and I saw this as the time to get cracking.

Ross and I were attending the meeting along with Greg W, Dan and Roy. Mick was going to meet us later as he had a work commitment to attend.

Roy was a "no show" but said he'd catch up later. We had lunch in a pub before the meeting and had a bit of a meeting ourselves. Greg W was very efficient in recording everything down. We started to allocate roles for everyone it was all a bit professional.

Something had been bugging me and I needed to get it out in the open. Were we all ok with H4H's being one of the charities? What was the problem with them?

One of the guys felt that the soldiers were paid to do a job, knew what they were signing up for and he didn't see why they should get extra support, he didn't in his job. At least he was honest, although I didn't agree with him, some of them young lads might not have much of a choice in life and joining the forces is a chance to learn a trade. Regardless of if you believe in the conflicts our nation is involved with or not, they are our country-men who have been through so much. I really didn't understand his attitude, but in fairness he was up for fundraising for both charities so we left it at that. To be honest he never did any fundraising and left the team in the not too distant future.

Skyline had been doing a fair bit of research and were looking for a £5,000 commitment from us. In their line of work people ask them to do things all the time, but when it comes to parting with cash suddenly back out, so I think it was only fair to ask us to front up. The cost of the trip would be about £4,000 each plus flights, wow that hit home big time.

After the meeting we met up with Mick in Soho, Roy was a "no show" I filled Mick in with the days events, I loved Micks enthusiasm, his glass was always half full.

The next thing to sort out was the date. October 2013 was looking favourable it gave us a fair bit of time to fundraise and the weather wouldn't be to hot or too cold. Greg W had some specific dates he wanted us to go, as he wanted his family to come over in the half-term. Some of the other guys were more interested in beating the snow in Chicago and half-term didn't come into the equation.

The biggest decision and the one that would keep coming up over the next twenty months was funding.

With quite a few charity challenges you raise money, offset the costs and the charity get the remainder. Now there is nothing wrong with that, as long as you tell people that's what you're doing, thousands of skydives etc are run this way. The London Marathon sells places to charities, which charities take out of the sponsorship money to pay for. I personally didn't want to do this on Route 66 nor did Mick or Ross. It was something we had discussed from the very beginning. With a trip costing over £40,000, you could end up raising no money for the charities. The first thing people say to you is, "oh you having a free holiday." I only wanted to answer that with no I'm not. Feelings really were running high on this, Mick and I were not going to participate if this was the case and this was very clear from the start. This same point came up time and time again as riders came in and then left, in fact it became quite tedious. I'm sure at this time some of the others would have preferred to offset the costs with donation money but we stuck to our guns. The big point that kept being stressed was we would get sponsorship from companies and we would all try harder to do so. All along I was thinking, start saving now Kevee because you're going to need it.

We had all been allocated roles, it was a bit like running a business at times I could see the sense in it but it did take a bit of the fun out of it. Ross was to be the chairman, I was pleased about that as he was my mate and if we had to have a chairman I would rather it be Ross, after all it was his idea from the start. Andy being a banker would open the bank accounts and keep tabs on everything, making sure everything was 100% right. I was going to be the link for The Willow Foundation as they are only around the corner. Everybody had a role, I can't remember what they all were and I'm not looking back through the minutes as it will take forever We needed to start training, going out as a team learning to ride together, this was a great idea, but something we never really achieved from day one. Looking back on the whole trip we never cycled at night before we started in Chicago, the closest we came was a 4 am start when we cycled to Brighton in September 2013. It made it more of a challenge when we hit the start line, the unknown certainly jumped up and grabbed us.

We had another meeting this time at my house, it was the beginning of April 2012, Roy never made it, he had become very quiet. I sensed things were not quite right as we all sat round the table. I think that although we were still confident about gaining sponsorship, others were starting to realize that they might have to dip into their own pockets. We needed to think about flights, which were about £600, Skyline were looking for a £5,000 deposit as well. This was going to be a crunch time for Route 66, the funny thing was we were still spending loads of time talking about writing to bike manufactures and cycle shops to try and get new bikes for the trip. I was quite happy with my bike, I couldn't see the sense in wasting time and effort trying to get something we already had, when what we should be doing was concentrating on organising charity events. Mick and Andy were very good at this side of things and had raised thousands in the past, whereas the rest of us needed to up our game.

A while after this meeting Greg W took the decision to pull out. I think the time and effort needed was going to impact on his family life and he was unhappy with that. From the groups point of view it meant we could move the trip forward a week and avoid the possible snow in Flagstaff!!!

We had other people interested, Hyphen was desperate to get involved, Mick had a family member called Kev (I'll call him little Kev, to many Kevs) and my son Casey was also dead keen to get involved. At this time we were talking about ten riders again just to give us a chance if anymore pulled out.

I spoke to Ross, I started to worry about big Dan, as he was a bit isolated now in Norwich and he also had a young family. What about Roy and Billy? Roy was very quiet, Billy really didn't want to pay for the whole trip, Andy was also keen not to spend too much of his own money, the trip could implode if more people pulled out. Ross asked the question on Facebook, it had to be done.

Big Dan as feared by me was going to have to pull out. The financial commitment was going to be too great for him, his family had to come first. I was gutted I really had a lot of time for Dan we had become great mates. Dan had been so instrumental in a lot of ways, he designed our logo, had forged our partnership with The Willow Foundation and started our Facebook page; he was just a genuinely fantastic bloke. He promised to stay in touch and help us out which he did all the way through. Mick said at the time to him, "your time will come Dan" and I'm sure it will. You were certainly missed mate of that you can be sure.

Chapter 3

Day One – We're On Our Way

We were in the RV's heading for the start, it was about 5am in the morning. Kenny had the music turned up and we were singing along, everyone was a bit excited to say the least. The crew thought the junction by the official start sign would be busy, so we had planned to pull up away from the start then cycle all together to the sign post, have a quick photo then we would be on our way. The crew had wanted to start early to miss the traffic and it was a fair point, being a Friday there was quite a bit of traffic about. I would have liked to start a bit later because it now meant to complete the challenge in seven days we would need to finish by about 6am next Friday morning and who would be about at that time to see us finish? We had discussed it together and the decision had been made, so here we were. All eight riders would cycle the first twenty miles together, this would be the only time we would do this until the last twenty miles of the trip next Friday, well that was the plan.

We pulled up about a quarter of a mile from the start. We all got our bikes out and were ready to rumble. Two years of planning, it could all be over in seven days. Sandra and Bernice were with us in their massive four by four, ready to start their own adventure. The crew were ready in the two RV'S. We rode to the official start line feeling anxious but excited let's hope nothing was going to go wrong.

As we turned on to Route 66 twenty yards from the start, the RV with James driving nearly had a collision with a car. The occupant of which wasn't very happy. He refused to move his car, he just needed to reverse about a foot but he wasn't having any of it. It was still a bit dark and eerie feeling. I took a bit of time out on my own I even smoked a cigar as I pondered on the thought, this was a good start. After about half an hour we finally could get going, the car driver finally realising he was probably late for work maybe and moved his mirror so we could continue, it was about 6:15am on Friday 4 October 2013.

The road wasn't too busy; most of the traffic was heading into town. We had a bit of a stop/start early ride with traffic lights then the road started to open out a bit and the pace picked up, I found myself in my usual place at the rear. It must have been the adrenaline rush the other guys were cracking out a pretty fast pace, but it wasn't consistent and I seem to ride better at a consistent pace. I was hanging on already hoping my cycling legs would kick in a lot sooner than they normally do on a multi-day ride. We were approaching the twenty-mile mark, this is where we would stop and just continue in pairs until we hit LA. What could go wrong now?

The crew had told us to use the toilets as little as possible as they didn't know how often we would need to empty them. With eight riders trying to hydrate as much as possible this can normally cause quite a bit of urinating. We were in a car park away from anyone and a couple of guys took a leak against a wall. Poor old Mark got in on the act only to turn round to see the Sherriff or some sort of officer, not looking very amused. We had the lecture of why are we doing this when you have two vehicles with toilets right beside you. Would you do this in England? What if a lady saw you? Ok fair comment and from now on we would be urinating in the RV or stopping at garages along the way.

Who was going to be the first two up for forty miles? Bazza had his hand up, as did Mick. It was a little strange as we were all partnered up really but that's how we started. Ross and Mark volunteered to go last, which I was surprised at; I thought those two would be chomping at the bit to get going. It was a decision that would later come back and haunt them time and time again. Dan and Andy would go after Bazza and Mick, that left Casey and I with the third slot and we really didn't mind what slot we had.

Mick did well keeping up with Barry, because out of all of us he really is a cyclist. We got to the first change over and Danny and Andy took over. I don't think anyone was going to sleep for two days we were all so excited. Barry was a bit miffed because he had trained the whole time prior to the trip with Danny and really wanted to cycle with him. I think Mick just wanted to cycle with everyone but the way it was set up in forty mile stints meant that this wouldn't happen. You would cock-up rest periods if you kept changing teams and we all needed rest periods.

Danny and Andy put a good shift in then it was Casey and I up next. It was early afternoon progress was going well. Andy said the wind had started to pick up a bit, I didn't take much notice it was about eighty-five degrees, it was our first proper ride and I was ready. We were somewhere near a place called Dwight and our 40 miles would finish near Lexington still in Illinois.

Oh my God, it was like getting hit in the face constantly with a cricket bat. The wind got worse and worse. Casey was pulling away from me and he kept asking me, "what's wrong dad?" I tried to tell him it was not a race and we had seven days to go plus the wind was killing me. He eased off a bit and we battled through but the last six miles were so tough in the end the support crew realised that the wind was proving a problem and pulled in front to try and help us out. This was a low point for me, if we had wind like this for seven days we would be in trouble.

We hit the rendezvous point with the forward RV. Ross and Mark were ready to unleash. Casey and I transferred to the forward bus, it was supposed to be our rest period but we were in no mood to sleep. I felt so deflated I had struggled big time, the wind had got the better of me, I was pleased Casey had kept in front but it was unfair on him, as I just couldn't pass to take a turn on the front.

Ross had arranged to have SIM cards for all of us so we could update progress regularly on Facebook and Twitter, it was free of charge, a great gesture. Unfortunately something went wrong and we couldn't use them. It looked like we would be eating a lot of McDonalds on the trip to take advantage of the free Wi-Fi. Those milkshakes they serve certainly helped a lot with recovery during the trip.

From what I have heard Ross and Mark's stint was really hot and windy and it took quite a bit out of them. They had never cycled together before and I suspect they were pushing each other hard. The time scale of seven days was paramount to Ross and Mark, whereas I was more concerned with completing the challenge; as I had said in my blogs, if it took eight days so be it.

I'm not too sure how Barry and Danny faired, but I have no doubt that it would have been fast. Andy and Mick cycled to the front bus where we were to take over and they looked ok. It was now late night on the Friday and as a team we were doing well. We set off and soon realised that the support bus wasn't exactly behind us. This was a bit worrying for me as this was always the plan, the RV would be with us 100% at night, as we were aware of what had happened to James Cracknell. We followed the orange arrows that were being placed by the front RV but it was proving very difficult to see them, the lights we had purchased were not up to the job of seeing them. The road we were on was in a bad way; it was a job to stay on the bike. We later found out Skyline had routed us around this section as it was deemed too dangerous to cycle on. We were definitely lost.

It was pitch black, it was a challenge all right. A big four by four was coming up behind us I didn't like the feel of this. It pulled up beside us as we cycled and wound down his window. "You boys ok? I think you lost your light," he handed me my backlight which must have bounced off. I took the light and thanked him as he put his foot down and sped off. I don't know what I had been thinking but I felt relieved, unfortunately I took my eye off the potholes below and took an almighty tumble. My elbow and knee coming off a bit worse for wear.

We cycled on a bit then thought we will have to back track, as we didn't have a clue where we were. I phoned the support vehicles, but got no reply; this wasn't a good first night. We got back to a sort of main road, the RV might now be in front of us this could be a long night. As if by magic the RV arrived, thank God for that. The rest of our section went well, the road surface was really bad and punctures were on my mind but we came through ok and we handed the batten over to Ross and Mark, the night air was starting to get a little cold and we told them to wrap up. We had something to eat and tried to get our heads down. Casey snuggled up with Bazza in the double bed, I hit the top bunk and I remember thinking to myself if I go to sleep then when I wake it will only be six days to go. I couldn't sleep my mind was ticking over, I worked out that I would be doing 16 stints and I had already done three so it wasn't too bad. My legs were feeling good, this was encouraging and my rear end was doing well. The keeping clean was a major concern of mine if you're getting hot and sweaty you really do need to pay attention to your under carriage, as any cyclist will tell you this is paramount to enjoying your cycling. I had come prepared with loads of wet wipes and Sudocrem and we had the on board shower.

Ross and Mark finished and Barry and Dan hit the road again. Ross and Mark looked cold and tired and they hit the sack pretty quickly. We had nearly completed our first 24 hours; by the time we hit the next changeover that would be it. We would have covered about 360 miles not bad and somewhere near target. Danny Boy was starting to feel the effects of the flu. Casey had had it before we came away as did I, Bernice and Sandra and it was horrible so how Dan was managing was beyond belief, one thing was for certain it would get worse before it would get better. The guys put in another good stint and as we approached the changeover, day one was complete. Let's hope the weather will be kind to us on day two.

Chapter 4

New Riders

It had been a hectic couple of months. Greg W had left followed by Dan. Little Kev was going to join but changed his mind. Big Kev was in, as was Casey so we still had eight.

Big Kev or Hyphen had been desperate to join from the start, he had been on L2P but like Greg W we hadn't cycled with him or had much to do with him. Myself, Ross and Mick had met him to talk through with him what we were looking for, but to be honest he did the talking. We couldn't get a word in, now I'm not one usually lost for words but this fellow could talk. He was a salesman, so I suppose you could say he sold himself well. He worked for a big car company who were owned by a big American firm who could potentially do this that and the other for us. As we left I remember Mick turning to me and saying, "That guy can Talk." He wasn't wrong!

Ross was dead nuts to get him on board, he was a good cyclist, well connected and so keen. Now I'm not a miserable bastard and I don't mean to sound like one, if you are a salesman you sell, that's what you do. My dad was a salesman and he would tell you whatever you wanted to hear to get a sale. Being well-connected means nothing to me, maybe that's why I'm not as successful as others, I like to deal with people not reputations. I went along with Hyphen as the others were keen and in fairness, if what he was saying he could deliver came true, the trip would prove successful.

Casey also came on board at this time, I was so pleased the lads wanted him; I kept out of the vote, which was only fair being a tad biased. I thought it would be good for Billy too, having a 19-year-old; someone more his age.

We were due another meeting so we all met up in London again. Roy was a no-show, we started to be a bit concerned by this. It ended up with Hyphen talking a lot about who needed to do what and I'm doing this. He was actually getting stuff sorted and had a big drive in him.

Hyphen left early and Casey was very quiet. Ross and Mick had a chat with him, after listening to the sales pitch by Hyphen, he just felt he couldn't offer much at this time with his degree and Uni Rugby going on. Mick and Ross gave him a cuddle and told him not to worry he would be a valuable member of the team and his amount of friends on Twitter and Facebook would come in very handy later on.

I was trying not to let the fact that Hyphen was winding me up come out too much. I wanted this trip to happen and didn't want to rock the boat, but I didn't like being told what I had to do and when.

I found this part of the whole experience the worst. We were a team of guys all equal in my eyes with valid points to make, that we might not all agree on, but it was all out in the open. We suddenly started having one-to-one emails and one-to-one phone calls. The Hyphen was getting money in though and was spreading the word, perhaps he was doing more than most, or were others doing as much and just not shouting about it? The point where I really lost the plot was after we had been to Mick's for a barbecue. Mick, Andy, Hyphen, myself and our wives attended. I spent four hours with the guy and two hours after I get home he sends me an email slagging Ross off about the website being shite and we need to take control of it etc. etc. Now Ross has been my mate for a long time, why didn't he say something when I was with him. He phoned me the next day, I lost my temper and I told him I was thinking of leaving because of his attitude, then I told him, actually it might be you who has to leave. We kind of sorted it out; he wasn't going to demand I answer his emails within 24 hours and would slow down a bit. I calmed down. I think his heart was in the right place, he just didn't think about who he was upsetting. He stopped ringing me one-to-one after this and concentrated on Ross and Mick. I knew it would only be a matter of time before he spat the dummy out again and this would prove to be right.

Oh it all sounds a bit moody, but things were moving on. I was signed up to do the Three Cities ride along with Casey, Ross, Mick and Andy. We just couldn't seem to get together to ride as a team. My own personnel view was if I was to ride with Casey on the trip, I needed to get out with him. Andy and Mick always rode together so that would leave Ross to ride with the Hyphen. We were looking forward to meeting up with Nathan again; he was a great rider and a smashing bloke. We had talked about him coming on board but Mick and Ross were concerned he might not be able to raise the money for the trip or for fundraising. I think we should have given him the option, as he would have been an asset cycling. Sue and Jacqui were also on the Three Cities trip, they could both cycle well. We had met them on the L2P trip and had kept in touch. Also Jamie and Rob were on Three Cities. Now those guys could motor, we sounded them out after the trip but they couldn't commit at the time, which was a shame. The first day was hard as I really had not been out on the bike, working seven days a week the two months prior. We had about two miles to go and I clipped Casey's wheel, Mick said it was a spectacular fall straight over the bars still attached to the bike. Jesus it hurt, without my helmet I might not be here to tell the tale, because my head took a hell of a bash. The road was busy with lorries going into the port at Harwich, so I felt very lucky indeed. We boarded the ferry, I had been looking forward to a couple of beers with my supper but the way my head was hurting I thought better of it. I'm not one for confined spaces and the thought of sleeping on the ferry hadn't appealed to me in the slightest, so I was amazed that I slept so well. I remember setting sail and the next thing I was aware of was the wakeup call of *"Don't worry be happy"* piped into the cabin.

I was a bit jaded the next day cycling to Amsterdam but it was a short sixty miles on the flat. Ross, Casey, Mick, Andy, Nathan, Rob, Jamie and myself stayed together and managed a beer stop or two on route. We arrived in

Amsterdam early and headed out for a few beers before dinner. We literally had dinner and headed back into town, which was about a two minute stroll away. It's nice sitting in Amsterdam watching the world go by, an early start beckoned so we didn't stay out as late as we would have liked. A couple of the team did stay out a bit later; no names will be given. The third day was always going to be tough, 112 miles after a night out in Amsterdam! We headed out together and Jamie hit the front, he pulled all eight of us along for a good few miles. Nathan decided to have a puncture, he had already had a couple, so decided to get the wheel checked out, the support vehicle was an hour behind Casey said he would wait with him. Ross, Jamie and Rob proved too strong for Andy, Mick and I and soon left us behind. Not content with 112 miles we decided to take a wrong turn and do an extra six miles, just to prove the old boys were stronger! Nathan must have had six punctures that day; every time he and Casey caught us it would happen again. We all managed to catch up for a beer later in the day and looked forward to completing day three. The group split nearing the end and Mick won't mind me saying he was struggling a bit. We saw our team leader Sally up ahead, she was encouraging us shouting, "Only five more to go." Mick was well pleased until I told him five more miles not minutes, he looked empty so for once I talked him in, rather than the other way around. It had been a hard day, many of the riders had been scooped up in the love bus, the lack of training or determination bringing them up short.

Day four. I seem to get stronger as we near the end of a trip it could be psychological, it could be everyone else is slowing down, it could be I have good endurance; who knows. I felt good the last day and hit the front of our eight riders for a fair old stint. It wasn't the same arriving in Brussels as it had been in Paris probably due to the square we arrived in being packed with people attending a jazz festival. (Not my cup of tea.) Still Sandra was there as always to see me in, little did she know at this time she would be cycling to Paris next year.

We again met some great people on this trip Sue, John, Laura, Mel, Luke, Emily and many more. The great thing these days, is that you can keep in touch on Facebook after the event, I find it a very useful tool.

I think it did us all a power of good, over 300 miles in four days, the second time we had done this sort of distance. We knew we had over 600 miles each to do on Route 66 in seven days and we needed to crack on a bit faster, we also had to sleep in a bus rather than a hotel, but we could do that. I think we all needed a break from emails, Facebook and the cost of the future trip now looking like a big sum of money, this trip helped us to focus on something else.

It had been Casey's first foray into cycling; he had only got the bike a few weeks before and had done about 30 miles. He's so fit he managed it fine, but his arse was killing him. He was out of the seat more than in it the last day and had learnt a valuable lesson. You need to train, not to get fit but to harden your rear end.

I look back on our trips to Paris and Brussels and they really have been life-changing for me. I met so many people who have become very close friends; people who have wanted to achieve personnel goals but also raise money for people less fortunate than themselves. My life style has got back on track; eating better, drinking less and more exercise. I miss rugby but my body doesn't, I can walk on Monday mornings these days. If I could just stop smoking again!

It can be a bit of a come down after a big adventure although another big adventure was only 17 months away. Route 66 was going to be awesome, I was sure of that now we just had to firstly get enough people involved, eight was good; ten would be better, The challenge might not be as intense with ten, less mileage or perhaps just treble up on stints to keep the same mileage. I was convinced in my heart others would pull out before we arrived in Chicago, I wasn't 100% sure of who, but it would happen in the not too distant future.

Chapter 5

Day Two - Rain Wind And A 45 Miler

I did not get much sleep, the air was still full of excitement. It was early in the morning and the old troopers Mick and Andy were on the road. Conditions looked a little better this morning, the roads seemed to be tarmac and it didn't look too cold. As always I was in a world of my own thinking we have had heat, wind, got lost and cold, what would today bring? Ross was still sleeping. Mark was having a chat with Casey and me. The mood was good we were on target for seven days and everyone seemed fairly fresh. The crew driving looked fresh; this would change as the trip went on. I don't think any of the crew in the back bus had slept yet and they were looking after us well, cooking all the time, they certainly wanted us all to eat. My diet seemed to be consisting of pasta, don't get me wrong I love pasta, but I am more of a potato lover. Chips could be hitting and would be hitting the diet very soon. The Americans do eat. I wonder what the percentage is of Americans who work in the food industry? In England when you cycle you pass by fields, hit a village with a shop maybe a pub. You might pass loads of houses going into a town, couple of shops even a parade with a takeaway on the end. Industrial sites you might pass, then a complex with all the big stores and a couple of fast food outlets, then more housing and so on. In America you might see a couple of houses then about twenty food outlets, a mile down the road a couple more houses then gas stations selling about twenty types of coffee plus food and then another twenty food outlets (mostly the same ones as a mile up the road) what is there percentage of food outlets to houses?

It seemed to be getting a little hilly, Andy and Mick pounding on. Mick was doing well on the hills overtaking Andy and really attacking them, then Andy would ride over the crest and fly past Mick on the downhill. They had both put a huge amount of training in at the gym and on the bike. Andy was a shadow of his former self, having lost two to three stone. He had knocked his regular pints of Guinness on the head and changed his diet a fair bit. Casey was keen to tell me that losing that much weight that quick is not always a good thing and Andy didn't seem to be as strong as Mick on the hills as he used to be, I was putting it down to Mick's training programme and his rugged determination, as to why he was stronger on the hills. One thing you notice on the bus following your fellow cyclists is the style. Bazza had a very solid style – no movement at all – meaning a good core strength, Andy also has a good style. Ross, Mark and Danny also look good but run a quicker cadence and move about a bit. Mick; well his style isn't his strong point, his hips were rotating a hell of a lot. I think Baz and Steve told him to drop his seat a little, which improved it somewhat. Personally I think he just grits his teeth and sticks everything he has into it, style not being high on his list just the mileage under the belt.

It had started to rain, not heavily, but the sky didn't look great. I started to get ready, what was I going to wear? It could get warmer or it could get cold and wet, at least with a support bus not far away you could call it up beside you like in the Tour de France and get a change of clothes.

The bus headed a couple of miles up the road so we could get the bikes off the rack and get ready for the changeover. We were in a place called Bourbon – in the state of Missouri – having travelled through St Louis. It was at this time we noticed something wasn't quite right with Marks bike. We had pulled into a garage a few miles earlier and reversed the RV in a bit of a tight spot. Unbeknown to us we had reversed into a sign post and Marks bike frame had come off a little worse for wear, the funny thing was Casey who had been asleep had woken when we hit it, looked out the window and gone back to sleep. Now he was telling us we had knocked the sign over! Mark took it really well, it was just one of those things, Ian had bought his bike along so the next chance he got he would put it together and Mark could ride it, in the meantime he was to use mine.

Mick and Andy arrived and we did the usual, well done chaps, what's it like, a quick cuddle and we were off.

Casey hit the front and I was hanging in on his wheel. I really wasn't giving him much help, I was fighting to keep the wheel so much I couldn't get past him to take a turn, it was much the same as yesterday. As soon as we hit any sort of undulation he would pull away, I know in my heart if I tried to stay with him I would end up getting an early flight home. He would constantly ease off and come back to me and ask, "You alright dad?" I was alright I just couldn't keep the pace, I felt I was at the back of the peloton, pedalling squares about to go out the back door. I think he realised this now and he started to do an excellent job of pacing me, I had the Garmin so he would just keep asking what speed are we at? What's our average? How far to go? He wanted to show the other guys how good he was but at the same time wanted to cycle with me. It's a funny thing, we have always been competitive I encouraged it in him from an early age. I remember training for the London Marathon in 2000, he was only about eight but would want to come for a run with me. I used to take him across the common where we lived for a couple of miles then drop him back and go and run another ten to fifteen miles. About five or six years ago that all changed and we would go out together and run about five miles and not unlike today's situation I would be hanging on. His answer to why I was struggling was because I had started smoking again, in fact this was to blame for any shortcomings I may have at any time. When we played rugby together he was amazed I could run round the pitch; he thinks I'm some sort of medical mystery, I do like to remind him the greatest rugby player ever in my mind, Serge Blanco smoked twenty a day.

Well back on the road we were making good progress, a bit less wind today.

Then the rain started, not too bad at first but getting progressively heavier. We both took a drink and had a bit of a chat whilst still moving. Casey wanted to really hit the last ten as fast as we could to get out of the rain and this seemed like a good idea. We had climbed or it felt like we had climbed a bit and now the road seemed a bit easier. We were heading into Cuba (not the country a small town) and hit traffic lights, it was stop and start, but when we could go we put the hammer down. We had a bit of confusion with the orange arrows and nearly ended up on the interstate, the bus saving us and putting us right. We had a good bit of road to finish on and the rain dried up, it was a shame the cycling shoes didn't, as nothing is worse than wet feet, well maybe a wet backside but both together, lovely, We finished our forty miles in Rolla and again don't ask me what it was like, as I can't recall.

Ross and Mark were up and ready to go we had a quick hello but they headed out pretty quick. Now for the challenge of a shower on the bus, would Kenny let us have five minutes before he moved on the answer was yes.

We had a bite to eat and tried to get our heads down for a bit. Casey likes a sleep and he was straight off. I wasn't really getting much sleep at this point, my body would tell me when I needed to, you eventually get to a point when you just shut down. I wasn't quite at this point yet but I knew after the upcoming night shift I would be back in the front bus and about an eight hour break should see me right.

Andy seemed to be the most organised rider. His clothes were all in the wardrobes in order, he would finish his cycle, eat and then sleep. Casey would eat and eat, sleep then eat. Mick and I were like a couple of teenagers defying your parents, we were not going to sleep, perhaps it was adrenaline, two years in the planning we didn't want to miss anything. Mick wasn't really eating enough and he will tell you himself it proved to be a big mistake. When you're doing forty-mile stints you need to be well fuelled before you start and well fuelled during the ride. After the ride is a critical time to get food and liquid inside you. Casey is my son but sometimes you would think he is the dad because he would be monitoring what I would eat and drink constantly. I certainly take on more water when I ride with him as I am usually behind so I drink when he does, and it does make a difference. It's a bit odd having to do what your son tells you, but I'm a great believer in taking on advice from others if it helps me out.

We hit the change over and Barry and Danny emerged from the front bus looking fresh (Dan looked like shit actually the flu kicking in big time). Ross and Mark were ready to get a big sleep in the front bus.

Not much happens on the bus, if you're awake you just sit with the others listen to a bit of music the time goes really quickly. This might not be the case after a couple more days, as fatigue would start to set in. I was worried before I left, that motion sickness might set in 24/7 on the move, I normally like to sit in the front of a car looking forward, never able to read. The bus seemed more like a train; it wasn't affecting me at all. The constant stops for fuel were great I could jump out grab a coffee and sneak off for a smoke. I like that being on my own for five minutes, it's pretty full on fourteen blokes on two RVS.

I was hoping for a decent road surface tonight with no wind and rain. Steve and Ian had said to me you and Casey have had it pretty rough so far, what with the wind, the road surface and the rain, it's nice to hear that in a way, because you think you are imagining it yourself. I personally thought Danny had it the worst with the flu, but he was still hammering it down the road with Bazza. We hit the next change over it was about 5pm maybe 6pm. Someone had told us it was flat all the way until Arizona, we had believed them, this was certainly not the case. We hadn't factored the wind or that we would encounter climbs. We knew we had to average 15mph to make seven days, but these factors and change over times coupled with getting lost every now and then, would mean our average speed would need to be a wee bit faster to make up for all the unforeseen time wasted.

I wasn't really worrying I could only go as fast as I could go, so if it took us longer that's what would happen.

Danny and Bazza put a really fast stint in, I wasn't sure if it was because they were embracing the challenge or Danny was just wanting to get it done so he could get back to bed. Trying to shake the flu off in these conditions was nigh on impossible.

The worst thing when you are cycling is thinking you're doing a certain distance and then being told you will have to go further. The forward bus had travelled an extra ten miles up the road, this was due to having to find a suitable place to park up. After the forward bus route marked a hundred and twenty miles it would park up and everyone would get a couple of hours sleep. So Mick and Andy were about 30 miles in when we pulled up beside them to tell them it's going to be another 15 rather than 10 miles, they took it fairly well but you could see this was going to put them on the limit, having pushed the pace thinking only another ten to go. It dawned on me that Casey and I were also going to have to do an extra five miles, Christ I was on the limit with 40-mile sessions never mind 45. We agreed we would hit twenty-two and a half then stop for two minutes to re-fuel.

Andy and Mick finished and looked pretty exhausted. We hit the road, the good news was it was tarmac not many holes and quite a nice ride. We had borrowed some better lights so we could see, the RV was sitting behind us, that gave you even more vision and the wind was not as bad as it had been. It was getting hilly but without the wind the hills didn't seem too bad. We were rolling up and down, I was tired but going a lot better than I had been. We stopped at half way and took on some sweets and drinks, Casey popped a gel, he swears by them, but the taste, in my opinion, was not worth the result, so I stuck to the Mars Bars. We got back in the saddle and continued, after about 38 miles I was getting mighty tired but I was in great spirits, if the remaining night rides were all like tonight it would be a fairly easy ride to Santa Monica, this may have been wishful thinking on my part.

We made it, Ross and Mark not quite ready to head off this time they must have had a good sleep. Good old Ian had a load of pizza cooked for Casey and I, he had realised that Casey could eat and eat. King Kenny always had a milky coffee at the ready, Skyline definitely knew how to keep us two happy.

We actually got in the double bed at the back and got some sleep. It is amazing how you can sleep when James is driving, I can only describe it as like being on a roller coaster, Left, right, left, right then your literally hitting the ceiling as you hit a bump in the road, the roads are crap in some places so you're up and down almost levitating at certain times. We were levitating and Casey is spark out, how the hell he didn't wake up I'll never know.

Our second day was done when I awoke it would be past 6.30am in the morning, we would have completed two lots of 24hrs. I was startled by my phone going off, I must have been in a really deep sleep, at first I thought it was my alarm for work then realising it was ringing I answered it. Bex my daughter was on the other end telling me she had done it, I really wasn't with it at all, she was very excited, I must confess I was not awake so she said she would call me later.

It was light out so I got up, all the crew were dead to the world. Lucky for me we were at a garage so I could go to the toilet in peace and get a coffee. I went for a stroll and called my daughter, I knew now she was phoning up to tell me she had completed The Willow Foundation 10 kilometre run at Hatfield House. I was so proud of her, some of her mates were going to do it with her but didn't, some of my mates said they would see her at the start but didn't. She went along with her Nan and Granddad wearing her Route 66 top and flew the flag for us while we were away, (thanks Pop) I was missing her badly but she was constantly in touch with us the whole way through.

Chapter 6

The Launch, A 10k and Half A Team

Things seemed to be still moving on, it was seventeen months to go and the trip now seemed to be clogging up my email account. What with Facebook and Twitter a whole new world was opening up. It was difficult trying to keep up with all that was going on, you add work into the equation and you realise just how much was going on.

We had organised a family fun day at my local pub The Crooked Billet, the landlady Julie and landlord Wally could not have been more helpful. We were charging a tenner for adults £2.50 for kids and under-fives free, our total ticket sales prior to the event was about ten. Included in the price was a barbecue, bouncy castle and a band. The band was costing over £500 so I was starting to panic a little as were the pub. My mate Gav was on the door and I can tell you no one got in for free, a few tried but he was having none of it and stayed at the task from about 1pm until let's say very late indeed. As it happens we made £720 after paying for the band, food and bouncy castle. The pub were very generous toward us and the staff fantastic. It pissed down, but we all danced the night away and consumed maybe a beer or two. It's a funny thing but I feel if you're giving people something for their hard earned cash it doesn't seem as bad as just asking for money, maybe that's where I go wrong, others I know wouldn't bat an eyelid badgering people but I find it really hard.

Mick and Andy had a whole list of things they were organising, quiz nights, Zumbathon, golf day and pitching up at the Ivor Apple Day! Mick does have an appetite for an event and is so enthusiastic, he had even made the effort to attend our fun day.

The Hyphen was doing well getting money on the Virgin page; he certainly had some connections. We had some merchandise manufactured, mugs and wristbands, Billy had sold a few items, Roy was still a bit quiet.

Mick and I had signed up for the Willow bike ride, it was taking place on 15 July 2012 we were taking on the 60 miler, I must admit I had a great day out, culminating in meeting Bob Wilson and his wife at the end. I really struggled all the way round. We stopped halfway and had a can of cola and I got worse and worse after this. Casey informed me when I saw him that this was a big mistake, when you see them drinking it on the tour its flat, the bubbles don't agree with you whilst exercising. He did go into a more thorough explanation but let's leave it at that.

The Olympic Games were on now and the amount of cyclists on the road seemed to be growing every time I went out, which wasn't too often really. I went along with Sandra to watch the Paralympics, what a fabulous day, first of all the park itself was breathtaking. The atmosphere unbelievable, everybody looked jolly and strangers were talking to each other. The athletes themselves were just remarkable people, overcoming disability to triumph in the greatest of sporting occasions, the triumph in my eyes having the dedication to get to the games. I was thinking about our challenge, to me this would be my Olympics, if I could complete it without letting everyone down that would be my gold medal, although I would settle for a cigar and a beer at the end.

Around about this time one of my oldest friends Gez joined up for the trip. This meant we were up to nine riders, it had been agreed we should up the riders to ten. I was really pleased to have him on board, we go back a long way together, we met when we both worked at Tesco part-time. It's funny in life how you meet some people and you stick with them through the years; not necessarily seeing each other every week, but when you do see them you pick up where you left off as if it were yesterday. Gez had done even less cycling than me and would have to get a proper road bike and some lycra. He met the guys and was in, we just needed to get him on Facebook, it wasn't something he used but his wife and children could bring him up to speed.

I seemed to be doing nothing else but visiting Facebook and reading emails. Looking back through all the correspondence that was going on it was really quite amusing. We seemed to be moaning a lot about who was doing things and trying to rally the guys who were very quiet. The older guys were pushing things on setting targets, the younger guys were not being so active but we would certainly need these guys to be active on the actual trip.

Mick had been communicating with a guy called Sam who was taking on a massive running challenge around the UK for Help for Hero's, he had asked him if he would be interested in joining the team, the answer was yes so our ranks were now starting to swell and at last we had enough riders on board that even if we had an injury we could complete the challenge, Sam also had a mate that was interested and it would help him out to have someone to train with so Neil was added to the party. As soon as Sam got time he would come down to meet us.

I had been interviewed by a local paper and a radio station; we had been planning an official launch date for some time in September so we tried to tie it in with the media for maximum exposure. I think some of the guys were still under the illusion that this trip would make them famous. It was a great challenge, but as I have said before many people take on far greater challenges and if you are a celebrity you are going to get the limelight. I wish people would have just been happy with a personal goal to me I was taking part with my son and friends and couldn't have been happier about that.

The launch date arrived, 24 September 2012. We had banners made up and met up at my local pub. The local press took photos and Heart Radio ran a loop of the interview on the news every hour. We boarded an old London bus and headed for the west end in London handing out leaflets along the way. Not all riders had made it due to various reasons so myself Mick, Andy,

Ross, Casey, Billy, Gez and the Hyphen would take on the task of riding around London in the pouring rain spreading the word. We got back on the bus looking like drowned rats hoping the weather in America wouldn't be this bad (ha little did we know), Sandra and Bernice had prepared a cream tea for us; how quintessentially British is that?

Next up for me was The Willow Foundation 10k held annually in the grounds of Hatfield House. I had attended the previous year as a spectator cheering on Sandra and Bex. I hadn't trained; well I had been out for a couple of short runs. My mate Fraser is a keen runner and was taking part, I said I would see him at the finish. There was a mass warm up which I chose not to get involved with deciding a cigar was order of the day for me. To my utter amazement I completed it in under an hour, completing it had been my main objective but I secretly hoped to do it in under an hour without stopping, job done.

We had organised a Halloween party at our rugby club. We had a great night but numbers could have been better. Maybe our friends were getting tired of fundraisers already, it could be a long slog to the start day if this was the case early on.

The next bombshell to drop was just around the corner. Roy had become very quiet he had moved and had been trying to set up a company, having left his job. He had yet to pay his deposit and I guessed something was a foot. I had a text explaining that without corporate sponsorship he would not be able to fund his trip.

Shit, this wasn't good he was our best cyclist and a really good guy. He was being honest with himself and thought it better to pull out now rather than nearer the time. It is a great shame when people pull out, especially if they have been in since the start. As a team we needed to pull together fast.

We were just getting over Roy leaving when Billy decided he couldn't afford the trip either, the whole thing was starting to implode. Andy who had also been a bit inactive put a post on Facebook which read, "Guys thought for the day – which is the stronger ideal: losing the core team or changing our approach to funding this event?"

If his plan was to put the cat amongst the pigeons it certainly had the desired effect. How many times was he going to bring this up? Mick was incensed, we all knew the ideal from the start, to raise as much money for the charities as we could and if we couldn't raise sponsorship to pay for the trip it was coming out of our pockets. Why was he doing this? Ross came back with the same as Mick and I, he knew from the start, as did Billy and Roy. If anyone reading this is thinking about doing their own charity challenge my advice would be to nail your objectives from the start, even get it written down so you're all singing from the same Hymn sheet. Whichever way you want to fund a trip is fine, but to avoid the confusion at a later date sort it before you move to far. So far we had raised about £3,000 we had been fundraising for a good six to eight months and had only twelve to go, do the maths it wasn't looking good. Andy was keen to offset some of the cost with donation money, the trip was going to cost in excess of 40k, if we went down this route the charities would owe us 37k! All our initial targets were going pear-shaped, we had wanted to attempt a Guinness world record, Ross had been looking into this and it was all a bit complex so that wasn't happening, We wanted media coverage on a national scale, this wasn't happening, we wanted a celebrity to climb aboard a bike with us, again no, we really wanted to raise £100,000, we had more chance of winning the lottery.

Mick was ready to pull out if we changed the goal posts and I was with him, Billy had left and we had to move on, we didn't have the time to dwell on this. Mick had said to him, "you will miss one of the best experiences of your life if you pull out now and would probably regret it for a long time," who knows if he has seen it this way.

It was proving to be very stressful at this time, I couldn't tell who was in and who was out. I decided I needed to join the gym, the weather was really bad and we looked set for having a hard winter ahead. Everyone was training apart from me, I had done a couple of big rides but couldn't get myself motivated to get out week in week out. I have always hated the gym, the thought of posing around with all the other posers did not appeal to me at all. I was thinking more swimming, squash and tennis. I was entitled to an induction session on the gym equipment so went along anyway. This is where I first met Kat; she put me through my paces and was interested in why I was joining the gym. She gave me a plan of what I needed to do, it was quite refreshing, I know a few personnel trainers and to be quite honest some of them are so in love with themselves it's a wonder they get any clients. I'm not saying all of them are like that and the longer I spent at the gym the more I realised that. Sometimes you hear them taking the piss out of their clients to other trainers and I don't think that is right, they seem to be more interested in the money and looking at themselves in the mirror, it's a pity the mirror doesn't show up shallowness! We're not all born beautiful and no matter how hard we try you can only lose so much weight and tone up so much, what is beautiful anyway? I didn't really start training that much before Christmas but Kat would have a massive input later on in me riding Route 66.

Chapter 7

Day Three – Endeavour To Persevere

What was day three going to bring? It had started early with my daughters phone call, I was in top form I had had a great sleep, used the lovely clean facilities at the garage and was on my second large dose of caffeine. The yanks do know how to make good coffee. The crew and Casey had now stirred and were starting to panic, as Andy and Mick were only twenty minutes down the road. The sun was shining, it was of course a little windy in your face by the look of it, my legs were feeling really good and I wasn't fatigued at all, I must have slept for a while; the first big sleep for two days.

We were now in Oklahoma having slept through the state of Kansas, today Casey and I would cycle to Tulsa and beyond. We were less than *24 hours from Tulsa*, in fact only about an hour and a half. Mick and Andy arrived looking a bit wind swept but they looked ok, ready for a sleep I thought. The road condition was good; it was quite a main road with a few vehicles about. The wind seemed to be picking up which was a surprise, we had realised by now that this could be a factor all the way to LA so we had better get used to it and get on with it. We seemed to be climbing a bit but this could have been my imagination, the wind or legs being tired I wasn't sure. When you're cycling toward these cities you get a bit excited you've seen these places on the TV and heard them mentioned in songs, you get back to England and people ask what was Tulsa like and I don't know, we just cycled through it. I was probably looking at Casey's wheel. The thing I remember most about Tulsa was turning left, we turned left and we had no wind, oh what a relief. Unfortunately after a few miles we turned right and the wind was back at us. We dug in deep and kept pushing ourselves; we seemed to skirt around Tulsa and were soon coming out the other side. We were nearing the end of the session and had a bit of a downhill, the bus had pulled in front of us and we jumped in for a tow, they could see we were behind them and stuck there foot down, we tried to hang in but we were hitting about 30mph, I lost them, then hit the wind and was down to about 10mph within fifty yards and cycling downhill! The changeover was at a garage, which meant coffee and food, I love American garages they are the lifeblood of a nation, gas, coffee and food what more do you need.

Ross and Mark were not quite ready to go, the crew were working on a bike for Mark. After the incident with his bike and not getting on very well with my bike, Ian had put his bike together to try and get Mark comfortable. It was all getting a bit on top of him at this time, his training had been interrupted with an operation, him and Ross were not enjoying the night riding and his pride and joy was looking a bit worse for wear having been cracked in half on the sign post from hell! It was a nice change to have six riders together for a while. It was about twenty minutes before they hit the road and they were chomping at the bit to get going. Me, Bazza and Casey had a nice sit on a bench and watched Danny try to make love to his foam roller. He was rolling up and down on top of it, he looked like he was trying to hump it, perhaps it was too much male company or was he just missing his wife Charlotte? Casey jumped in and had a go, the two of them took it turns rolling up and down and crying out in pain, "Do you want to have a go Dad?" Ha I didn't think so, if I want a warm down I could walk over to get another coffee that would sort me out.

Ross and Mark were flying along, heads down and thrashing out a good speed. Ross was hitting the front a lot today and leaving Mark behind a bit, Ross was intent on keeping the speed high and not realising Mark was dropping off a fair bit. Casey was a lot faster than me but never strayed out of site, I used to tell him to go and attack the hills which he would but he would always ease off and keep on pulling me up. It was a great atmosphere on the bus today the sun was still out and we were doing ok, on time maybe, slipping back a little but holding our own.

It was like a Chinese laundry on the RV, every time you turned your head it ended up in someone's smelly wet kit. Lycra was hanging out from every window, any passing convertible car would have got a good old whiff of stale sweat mixed with chamois and sudacrem, nice. We had passed the guys and pulled up further along the route, we took advantage of this down time by laying all our damp lycra along a grass verge. It didn't work, some of this would have to go in a bin liner to be dealt with later, I forgot I had put this stuff in a bin liner for a number of days having thrown the bag on the shelf over the drivers area, I should apologise for this now to the crew as that's where they slept most of the time. I hope they didn't mistake the bin liner for a pillow at any point that could have been nasty. The boys passed us and we gathered the remainder of the said laundry and headed off after them. On a day like today we would not sit behind the riders but keep overtaking them and then stop ready to take a few action shots.

We hadn't managed to meet up with Sandra and Bernice for some reason, they didn't know where they were, sometimes we didn't know where we were, but today they drove up behind us. It was good to see them they smelt nice, what they thought of us heaven only knows. I gave Sandra a quick tour of the bus, she was very impressed! We did have all the windows and doors open so she couldn't really appreciate the full essence of the experience. Ross and Mark came into view and started the climb towards us they were a lot closer together now. They upped the pace Ross must have been eager to reach the top and see Bernice, Mark looked extremely pleased as well, they both soon didn't seem so pleased when we told them it wasn't the change over and they had another three miles to go! That is a killer when you think you have made it to the end of a shift and then having to stretch it out, Mick and Andy know all about that, Ross and Mark only had to look at their computers to see they were short on mileage though.

I jumped in the car with Sandra a nice three miles in luxury to the changeover point. Casey got some more clothes from the car; it is very handy having an extra vehicle to carry all your excess luggage.

Bazza was doing well, the only thing he was worrying about was the state of his Rapha lycra, not the fact it was damp, but if it had any creases in it. Danny was not looking well, the damp conditions putting pay to any chance of the manflu disappearing, if anything it was getting worse I was seriously wondering if he should be getting on that bike at all.

We pulled in at a garage the bus in front of us. The girls treated us to a coffee and a box of Crispy Crèmes, ah we were living the life of luxury. Ross and Mark pulled in and Dan and Baz hit the road, we grabbed another coffee and chewed the fat for a while before saying our goodbyes to the girls and boarding the bus. The jammy bastards Danny and Bazza were having a hell of a start about six miles downhill and Ross and Mark were definitely pointing this fact out. Casey and I should have been getting some shuteye but we were buzzing and not in the mood. Ross jumped into his favoured top bunk whilst Mark decided we needed a bit of Johnny Cash singing, *"The Ring of Fire"*, was it a subliminal message he was sending out. It was about this time Casey got the video camera out and as if by magic The Rollin Stones classic *"Get Your Kicks On Route 66"* came on the stereo. This was the time we recorded our infamous video and the less said about that the better!

Day three was turning out to be a real good day, I was almost eager to get back on the bike.

I was missing social media a lot more than I thought I would. You really don't appreciate how much you use things like Twitter and Facebook until you can't. We could have put our roaming on but that can be extremely expensive, so free WIFI stops were the way to go. Whenever we would get to a McDonalds or a diner, the lads would be straight on their phones, the funny thing was I was more interested in eating and having a smoke so by the time I logged myself in it was time to go. I probably had done enough of the talking prior to the trip starting so it was good to get the other guys updating things, although it was a bit sporadic. The girls lucky enough were staying in Motels so they could upload our progress daily as long as it didn't interfere with their evening glass of wine.

The rest of the day went pretty well we met with the first RV, Andy, Mick and the crew all looked pretty clean as they had all taken a shower and seemed very happy about that fact. I hadn't got my head down much all day, I was working on the principle don't sleep too much and eat loads during the day and after the night ride I would be ready to crash for a few hours. It was getting near to our turn but we seemed to have lost Andy and Mick. We had come through a town and figured they must have missed a turn at a set of lights. It was getting dark now and we needed to find them, we backtracked as did they and eventually we met them. Andy needed to re stock his drinks and change his clothes. Mick had that look of, oh this means our stint is going to be longer now and he was right they ended up doing about 51 miles. That is a long ride when fatigue is starting to set in.

We were in good form ready for our night ride; we were near a place called El Reno, we would end up just short of Hydro, passing Spur on the way. It is difficult to go into much detail about these places as it was dark and you are concentrating on cycling, maybe I shall return one day and spend some time looking around. I can't say I was enjoying the night ride as much as the daytime ride but it was ok. We had Steve driving behind us and he was staying right with us. He had said this was a long section with no towns and no turns off so we shouldn't get lost tonight. It was very dark. Every now and then we would pass a few houses set back from the road. Most of America seemed to go to bed about ten o'clock, it was deserted. We stopped to take a quick drink as we had been pushing hard, Steve asked us if we had seen the Coyote just beside the road eating its supper? Luckily enough we had missed that. Apparently I had nearly ran over a skunk which had had its tail up ready to give me a squirt of something, maybe it had smelt me and thought better of it!

We pushed on and a house was looming set back from the road on the left hand side, I heard a dog barking, as we passed the drive this dog came flying out and nearly had my foot, Bloody hell the pace went up pretty quick, Casey was gone like the wind. Now I love dogs and I have never been frightened of them, but over the course of the next two hours that was to change forever. Every time we would come near a house the barking would start sometimes you couldn't see the house so you didn't know which way they were coming left or right. It might be one, two, or three dogs. Can you imagine three dogs chasing you down the road? Your foot was clipped in so you couldn't kick them. I reckon I would have given Mark Cavendish a run for his money with my sprinting that night. In the road were these things that looked like mini dinosaurs running around so you would have to slalom around those, the skunks were all over the place with tails raised high and the bloody dogs were like a tag team running after you, if you were really lucky you could get a glimpse of a set of eyes glaring out of a bush and it wasn't one of the lads taking a leak. Casey didn't seem to be getting very far in front of me tonight he was sticking with his dad, was he looking after me or feeling safer beside me? I was bloody glad to finish that night. To the people who told us we hadn't trained enough at night and we should have been cycling as a team of eight around North Weald aerodrome to practise, I say how the hell would that have prepared us for tonight? Ross and Mark were getting ready to go, Mark wasn't looking comfortable he really didn't like dogs at all. A car pulled up beside us – bearing in mind we are in the middle of nowhere about nine blokes standing outside an RV – it was a young girl asking if we needed any help, can you imagine that happening in England she would have just passed by with the doors and windows locked and who would have blamed her. I would like to thank her anyway what a nice gesture. We had something to eat and got our heads down.

I don't really know what went on the rest of the night as I managed to get a couple of hours sleep. The dog problem remained persistent and Mark got attacked. Apparently he was severely shaken and had to climb off the bike. Big Bazza didn't want to leave Ross out on his own so jumped on his bike to do the last ten miles with him. It was a good thing to do and showed the team spirit. Apparently three dogs had attacked the RV as well during the night things were definitely livening up. Barry and Dan had the next stint, which took us up to the front RV and the early morning of day four. We had also had a discussion on changing the stints from forty to thirty miles, Ross and Mark seemed quite keen, I had been counting my stints down in my head this would mean shorter goes but more of them, in the next breath we were getting moaned at about taking too long over change overs, surely that would mean more time spent at change overs? I was just going to go with the flow. Andy and Mick were on the road expecting to do thirty miles. A message came back from the front RV that Bal and Dan were sticking to the original plan and wanted their fair share of sleep so that put an end to that. What would day four bring surely we had weathered the storm?

Chapter 8

The Realities Of Not Achieving

Time was ticking on and as I have stated before we really were not on track to achieve what we had set out to do. I was beginning to feel like I never wanted to do a charity challenge again. I had people telling me I had to do certain things, I wasn't really getting on with everybody, we had to cancel a fundraiser due to lack of ticket sales. I was beginning to feel like I didn't have that many friends.

I had a great Christmas with my Mother, Father and sisters all coming to our house. I popped down to Cornwall, which I love to see Sandra's Mother and Father and sister, I was now refreshed and ready to start training albeit in a gym as the weather was crap.

I booked in on a spinning class, our instructor was Kat and she pushed us really hard, to my utter amazement I really enjoyed it and I signed up for the next week. Ross, Sandra, Bernice and Casey all came along next week it was good fun all doing it together. Kat had said come to the circuits before spinning it would be good for my core strength so I had, Ross was doing his own stuff in the gym but a couple of weeks later realised that group training pushed you harder. So for two hours every Saturday morning I would push myself to the limit or rather Kat would. I can't really explain how much I was enjoying it, I started to spin Tuesday and Thursday nights sometimes have a swim on Friday then the Saturday mornings. I had thought long and hard about the gym; the cost being about £150 a month, for Sandra and me it's a lot of money. On reflection I wasn't going out for a beer at all, my mates were wondering what had happened to me, even the rugby club were sending out search parties. I was saving a small fortune, I often would go to Twickenham for international matches and this would cost about £200 for a day what with train fare, lunch, ticket, supper and a few beers thrown in. I was losing weight and feeling really good everyone was telling me how young I looked, perhaps the gym was a good idea after all. I was saving money and feeling better for it. The weather was bad with loads of snow on the ground, I had sent my blokes home from work as we couldn't get on, one of them decided to go sledging with teenagers and broke his ribs, work was going to be tough when we started back.

I signed up to do another London to Paris, this time with Sandra. I thought the mileage and multi day ride would be good preparation. The thing about working out all week in the rain and snow is when Ross or whoever wants you to go out for a ride at the weekend you don't really fancy it, you can only take so much cold and I was so tired from work, the nice warm gym followed by a sauna was very appealing. Casey was impressed with Kat and he knows a thing or two about training, anyone who could keep me motivated was a good thing. The gym was a good release for me and I could see the results week by week. I was taking porridge to work to eat at break; I seemed to be a changed man. So much had happened in my life over the previous twelve months, none of it relevant to the challenge or this story but I had vowed to myself from now on I would be a different person.

Back to the mundane stuff of how the team was progressing and who was in and who was out. I'm having to look back through all the endless text messages, emails and Facebook posts to try and remember what was happening at this time. I really don't want to bore you with every intricate detail I find if I'm reading something like that you can get disinterested very quickly.

Basically the team was in disarray from the end of November 2012 until about March 2013. Mark had come in and he seemed like a good fella. We met him at Hyphen's house for a team meeting which went ok apart from the resurfacing of the 'how to fund the trip.' I wish they would give it a rest. Sam had decided he wasn't going to do the trip after the success of his run he had a lot of offers on the table, anyway he was gone. His mate Neil who none of us had ever spoke with had also left. My mate Gez also decided to leave which I found very hard, I know Gez better than most and the financial commitment was playing on his mind, the thing with Gez is his family always come first, no matter what and I can completely understand that. He felt he should be spending the money not on himself, but on his family he had hoped on some financial backing, which was not going to happen so he had to say no to us, which was fair enough.

It was about this time Danny joined the party, with all the negative stuff going on this was the one bit of good news. I knew his brothers and I knew he would be a great addition to the team; he was fit, excited and a fellow builder, so he should merge in pretty well. We planned a social in London at the Sports Café in Haymarket, it was a great get together, a time to relax and get to know the new members. Mark and I had a good chat and he was very honest; he told me he wanted to raise money for the charities but his main objective was completing the ride, that's what he wanted to do. I admired his honesty but thought Mick probably wouldn't see it quite that way, the less said the better. We were running out of options for riders and Mick demanding new riders must still commit to raising £10,000 wasn't realistic, we hadn't raised that much between us all.

Around this time Hyphen decided to leave, him Ross and Mick had been falling out over something on email and for once in my life I kept my mouth shut and let them sort it out. It resulted in Hyphen sending Mick an email resigning from the group. I have never seen the actual email, as Mick wouldn't show it to me, perhaps he had his reasons. The upshot was he left, in fairness he put a lot of effort into the group and although I did not see eye to eye with him on numerous things I think his heart was in the right place, in different circumstances we may have got on better.

So a roll call, Ross, Mick, Andy, Casey, Danny, Mark and me, the magnificent seven, we needed another rider. It looked like ten riders was out of the equation, I would certainly settle for eight, seven would be a real struggle.

Just over seven months to go and we really had not got the charity money coming in, what else could we do. Mick had organised a comedy night and it turned out to be a great success his group of friends really did attend everything he put on. We were starting to pin our hopes on the ball if we could raise £6,000 or possibly £8,000 that could pull our fundraising round and double what we had already raised. We had to face facts £100,000 was a bold target and we were nowhere near it. I had been to The Willow top tips seminar for the second year running, they were such a nice bunch of people I didn't want to let them down I had to try harder to get our challenge out there. I had started to write a weekly blog and to my amazement people were actually reading it. Andy was going to originally do the blog but for one reason or another had not got round to doing it, we had wasted over a year by not doing it so I jumped in and took it on. The Facebook page was growing in popularity and the blog was getting around a thousand views within weeks of starting. If my daughter and Casey shared it with their friends it went through the roof sometimes hitting two thousand. We probably didn't share it enough, if every team member shared it every week it would have got bigger and bigger but the guys were very sporadic in doing this, it did disappoint me a little I was spending hours trying to make it interesting but I wasn't going to push it as I didn't like to be pushed myself. Mick was chasing everyone to do things and getting a bit pissed off with people not. Ross was really busy at work but still wanted to take a lot of things on. The website was so out of date all the time but we had Mark now who's work was something to do with websites, but even he couldn't sort it out. Casey was nearing the end of his degree and his Uni rugby career. Andy was off the radar; work commitments keeping him out of the loop. Danny on the other hand was organising a clay pigeon shoot and a space at the local village day. Ross had been out with Danny on the bike and said he was a top rider so good news there. This was also the time when Mark informed us he was to have a hernia operation, crikey would he be ok for the ride? What chance would we have with only six?

We still hadn't signed any contract with Skyline, Ross was the link with Sally at Skyline, I was desperate to phone her up for a chat, I had always got on well with her but I didn't want to tread on any toes.

Was it just us or are all charity events plagued with utter turmoil at times? I suppose it is like running a business one minute you are up the next you are on your knees, you just have to pick yourself up and keep going. We may get times on the trip when the chips are down and we won't be able to throw in the towel then and jump on the plane home, we will have to see it through to the end.

On the upside at this time Sandra was doing well at the gym, Bex was joining her as well so the whole family was training; who would have thought it years ago.

I was busy at work, very busy. I was working on a major garden project and we had an open garden day coming up. Going by the previous year seven hundred people would be coming to look at this garden and we couldn't get the final plans off the designer, I had a feeling the next three months, I would be working seven days a week for most of it and would prove to be right, what about my training? It was going to go out the window very shortly, I feared.

Chapter 9

Day Four – And All Is Well

I had managed to get a bit more sleep and was looking forward to today. We should reach the midpoint of Route 66 and could gauge for real how we were doing for time. It was a glorious day, still a little fresh as it was early, but it looked like the sun was going to shine all day. The dogs never seemed to be too bad during the day and you could usually see them if they were coming for you. Mick had struggled a bit on the early rides due to the fact he wasn't eating enough, he certainly had taken it on board and was well fuelled these days. Andy was plodding along quite happily, in fact if he was cold or hot or thirsty or hungry he would just pull over and call the RV up; never mind he always had a bag on his back, we think it was his comforter a bit like an infant has a blanket or a cuddly toy, nothing ever went in the bag or came out of it! A message had come through, the van ahead was about ten miles further on again than anticipated which meant an extra five miles per group. The crew thought they would leave it till later to tell Mick and Andy, I emphasized that they better tell them as soon as possible, Mick wasn't going to like it. The previous day Mark and Ross had decided that they wanted to do shorter rides, so a decision had been made to do this. Mick and Andy were under the impression when they started that they were only going to do thirty miles, hence they had been going hell for leather to get it done quickly. We had already informed them that this had changed as Danny and Bazza didn't want to change it, so they were already on the limit to hit forty. Andy wanted something from the van, Mick pulled up beside me. I explained Skyline wanted him to do an extra five miles and he answered, "Skyline can fuck off, we done fifty-one last night and forty-five the day before, we started this ride only going to do thirty then it was upped to forty, I'm knackered Kev." It was a fair comment if you know when your finishing and then the goal posts get extended sometimes you can't do it. Lucky Bazza and Danny said no worries we will stick the extra ten in. It saved an argument and we could continue without fuss.

We were talking about the fact we had hardly any mechanicals Casey stressing he had never had a puncture since he got his bike (well done Case).

We swapped over and we were on our way, we had met a guy called Kevin who was cycling coast to coast and he had tagged on with Andy and Mick. He asked to cycle with us for a bit, we chatted away for half an hour then Casey decided to put the pace on, I dropped in behind and Kevin caught my wheel it was good fun but short lived. Casey had picked up a puncture after just bragging about not having one. We told Kevin to push on follow the orange arrows and we would see him later. I went to get my spare tubes out of my saddlebag and then realised the crew had taken it off last night to fit the bikes on the rack. We waited about half an hour before the crew arrived, we got sorted and were soon up and running. We had to do a bit of a detour on a road that can only be described as truly amazing. No traffic at all a good surface and rolling up and down and up and down. The bus left us and we were on our own, so this was Texas. It was big. Now that we had left the side of the Interstate we could really enjoy the solitude.

We rolled on, stopping on a bridge to take photos and re-hydrate. As a father with my son it doesn't get much better than this, we were talking and laughing about the previous night's dog attacks. We would race each other on the hills I was certainly not winning, but I like to think competing. It was getting hot and we had to keep drinking, the only thing was we couldn't see the RV and we were running out of water. It was now like being in an old western movie, we were down to our last quarter of a canteen of water, where was the cavalry? The road changed a little, a few big old Lorries joining from a side road our peace and tranquillity shattered, it had been a fabulous section so far. We did need some water and in the distance what looked like the RV, we were saved. I took Casey's arm and we rode in together. Big Bazz fearing the worst had some flat coke ready for me to ingest and it went down a treat. We saddled up again to complete our section the road coming to an end and a left turn took us onto a busier road. That was by far our most enjoyable ride we were really buzzing, getting stronger as the week went on. Our next ride would start after the halfway point the week was going by quickly now.

Casey couldn't get enough, he wanted to jump in with Bazza and Danny to time trial the ten miles in. Off they set. Casey hanging in at the back as the boys stuck a relentless pace in, they dropped him off a bit but he came roaring back and hit the front, it was short lived, Bazza knowing a few pictures were going to be taken, wanted to get out front to show off his Rapha clothing, Danny Boy was having none of it and got his snarling snot ridden face on the front, no poxy man flu would keep him out of shot. Casey was just happy to have his body in the photo his pained expression of trying to keep up would have smashed any camera. One of the photos of the trip was captured and really tells the tale of the effort needed for this trip. In the end it was only seven and a half miles and the guys did us proud.

Ross and Mark took over and were going to put a fifty-mile stint in. I wasn't sure about this it seemed a bit crazy. Ross is and hopefully always will be, one of my best friends but he was acting in a way I have never seen before. Yesterday he wanted to cut the mileage to thirty, today he wanted to put a fifty in, what was happening? I thought about it then it hit me, Ross and Mark had been complaining about riding the graveyard stint (as they called it) every night and how it wasn't fair, by changing the length of the ride they would alter the start times. It was a bold move to push fifty miles; we were all on the limit at forty. They must have forgotten we were travelling through time zones and putting a long session in would only put them back where they started. The thing is if you are doing a 24hr challenge it doesn't really matter what stint you are on you will sleep when you need to and Mark and Ross didn't seem to be having trouble sleeping from what I could see. The time was rolling on at least an hour a day so they should have let it be. The really ironic thing is they choose that shift by jumping in the front bus on the first day and wanting to start last. Later in the week Andy and Mick would moan that they would have liked to have rode a bit more in the middle of the day, if only they had talked to each other! I couldn't care less what time I was riding you had to do what you had to do.

We had transferred to the front bus, but were in no mood to sleep. I was really enjoying the trip now, I had struggled for pace the first couple of days but was feeling so relaxed now. My training must have been better than I thought. I was lighter and stronger, just not faster. We pulled up for fuel and jumped in with Bernice and Sandra we thought we might have a comfortable ride to the midpoint and I needed some female company. We arrived at the midpoint, it had been decided we were going to wait for the guys then have an hour rest all together and have a meal. All good plans can be put to rest as the diner was shutting. We found a garage up the road and stuffed our faces with subs and chicken. We returned to the midpoint and waited for the others, it was starting to get dark now. The boys pulled up and it was a great feeling we had made it half way. We took loads of photos and contemplated on what we had achieved so far. We were a little behind schedule, but did it really matter? Who wanted to finish at 6.30am in Santa Monica? Skyline did for one as the RV's were booked back at 9am that day, madness if you asked me, Ross and Mark did because that was the seven day cut off time. They started having discussions about getting a head of the riders and starting a bit early to make up all the time we had lost wasting twenty minutes every change over, I would rather have the van with me at night not ten miles up the road getting bikes ready. Were we in a race? What if one of those dogs got hold of someone?

Keep smiling Kevee and do what you have to do, I told Casey the same. We could have a moan to each other on the bike if needed but I wasn't going to let anything get to me I came here to ride Route 66 and that was what I was going to do.

Anyway we all had a good break at the midpoint, people needed that hour or so just to take a few photos and to know we had broken the back of it. We still had a lot to do but surely it would be easier in the desert wouldn't it?

The next issue to arise came in the form of a bombshell and would cause an awful lot of bad feeling over the next day or two. Greg informed me that Ross had decided we were going to miss out the Santa Fe climb and take the shorter route along the flat, this would save us sixty odd miles and a fair bit of time. I was gobsmacked, for one we had had no team discussion and why would we do this?

Now both routes are classed as Historic Route 66, but one is more historic than the other and is a real test of endurance. The other thing was we were always going to do the climb, I didn't want to come home and all my cycling mates ask us, how did you find the climb to Santa Fe and then have to tell them we missed it out. The crew were knackered and the thought of staying up all night planning a new route wasn't really appealing to them either. I needed to speak to the other riders before any decision could be made I was pretty confident that the other riders would not want to take the short cut.

Mick and Andy had another seventeen miles to go then we were up again. The old warriors had enjoyed their break at the midpoint. When we changed over we spoke about missing Santa Fe out, they were having none of it as I suspected. Casey and I would cycle most of the night weaving beside the interstate with a short section on it, we didn't enjoy that at all. It was fairly windy, fairly cold and nothing too exciting happened. Casey saw a snake and warned me, I'm not a great lover of snakes, we had seen a lot less than I thought we would but the desert was looming! We were heading to Tucumcari in New Mexico leaving Texas behind us. The wind always seemed worse next to an interstate, I don't know why but it is. You can see the interstate traffic a fair way off at night and you think that looks flat, the old road doesn't seem to follow the same line though and you're going up over it under it and round the mountain beside it. We cycled into Tucumcari cold and quite tired ready for a Kenny coffee and an Ian Pizza. Tucumcari was a real old style Route 66 town, I would love to have spent some time there but we cycled on and changed over on the outskirts, it's a pity I hadn't rang Sandra because her and Bernice had a motel room in the town we could have had a nice hot shower. Ross and Mark looked tired after there earlier fifty mile stint, this would be a hard ride tonight the wind was really strong.

It had taken a fair bit out of us tonight and I was ready for a rest, we chatted to the crew for a while then Bazz got up and I told him about the change in plan. He wasn't very happy either, Dan sort of stirred a bit, he looked painfully ill with the flu but he managed to say he didn't want to change either. Kenny got on the phone to Greg and told him that none of us wanted to change the route so stick to the original plan. That was that really six out of eight was the majority so it was good news we would do the original route as planned.

Fourteen blokes all on the limit you kind of know the stress levels would go up a little during the course of the week. The sleep deprivation; being hot one minute freezing the next, then having to smell the other blokes damp clothing, things were definitely getting the better of some. I drifted off to sleep, Ross and Mark finished and Bal and Dan headed out. I think during the night Dan had to come in, he was completely wiped out with the flu I was kind of half awake. When I woke we were just coming up to the front vehicle. Barry had been on the interstate on his own on a section that bikes were not allowed on so the bus had scooped him up and took him to the end of the interstate section where we were now. It was all happening at the moment. Ross and Mark had got really cold on their stint and you could still feel the cold coming out of Ross's legs. He jumped straight into the top bunk when I got out and we wrapped him up in sleeping bags.

The sun was just coming up it was a beautiful coloured sky; Andy and Mick would start the assent to Santa Fe. What would day five bring to the party, it was later to be known as 'Tetchy Tuesday" the reasons for this would soon become apparent.

Chapter 10

And Then There Were Eight

Time was really pushing on now and we hadn't had much good news of late. Ross had some news from Breitling, they had given him a thousand pounds to help us fund the trip. This was great news, was it to be the start of our corporate sponsorship at last, not really but we were so grateful to them.

Still it was a job well done, Ross and Hyphen before he left had put a lot of time and effort into corporate stuff and I should take my hat off because it was better than I thought we would do.

We were still a man down we needed to get someone in quick. People usually have things booked up a year in advance so seven months might be cutting it fine especially with the now confirmed costs. Many names were getting thrown around, Danny putting forward his mate Barry. He lived nearby so I went along with Ross and met him at a local pub along with Danny. Well this guy was the opposite too others we had met in the past playing himself down quite a bit as far as cycling was concerned. He did seem to know a bit about The Tour

The open day at work came and went and a week later Sandra and I were up at 4am on our way to Crystal Palace for the start of our London to Paris trip.

The thought of doing the trip with Sandra really excited me she had trained hard to get ready for this. We were doing the trip with Skyline again so I knew everything would be taken care of. We got to the start and I was pleased to see James was in charge I got on well with him. It was quite a small group only about eighty, we headed off at a relaxed pace. The weather didn't look too bright, I needed to train in all weathers for Route 66 so we would have to suck it and see.

We had a good first day in the rolling Kent countryside, Sandra cramped up a fair bit after lunch and struggled for an hour or so, we cracked on again then with about seven miles to go I hit a pot hole and had a puncture. I fixed the puncture then went to ride on and realized I had punctured the back wheel as well. Loads of riders had cycled past so now we ended up last. We still made the boat in plenty of time.

By the time we hit the hotel about 11pm Sandra was very tired, she showered and went to bed. I was felling quite good so met up with a few of the fellow cyclists and crew and hit the bar.

Day two was a gruelling wet day and the last hour or so was quite tough for Sandra, her right quad giving her some trouble. The thing I was noticing was it was harder to be near the back of the bunch rather than at the front simply due to the longer time spent in the saddle.

de France and The Classics which was nice, as all the others on the trip were really not into road racing. He seemed like a really nice chap but I remember coming away from there saying to Ross, "Do you think he cycles much?" How wrong can you be, he was going to prove to be a very valuable member of the team on the trip. The other guys said lets go for it so he was in. Getting Danny involved had been a great move, he was so enthusiastic, a great rider and now he had introduced us to Barry or Big Bazza as he became known.

The spirit in the team was really good at this time we had events planned by all team members and we were working on the ball. In my mind I was focused on the fact that I needed to get my head down at work to help pay for my trip. Unlucky for me the designer that we work for kept changing the plans on what we were constructing. She also kept adding things in, all for a deadline that I was struggling to keep. It's the old moving the goal posts routine again, you think you have so much to do then its doubled. The problem for me was I needed to train on the bike, but you know what its like when you get up its easier to drive to work especially if your putting ten to twelve hour shifts in. The guys who were working with me wouldn't work weekends so I ended up working six or seven days a week for about two months, I was shattered but still made it to the gym. Sometimes I would go to the gym Saturday mornings then back to work for the afternoon.

I was pinning my hopes on my London to Paris trip, I would be able to get a few solid miles in my legs and that could be my springboard to my training in earnest.

Its lovely to see total strangers teaming up and helping each other out, I met some great characters most notably Geoff a retired policeman and Hans. It was a pleasure to meet these guys, Hans having had all sorts of cancers –four in total – but insisting if you sat at home and moaned about it that would be the end of him. Life was too short you had to enjoy it and we certainly enjoyed it, drinking all sorts of things together in the evenings.

Day three was tough Sandra was struggling now with her leg and I was getting concerned as to whether she would make it, but she battled on knowing that it would only be one day to go if she got through today. It was a day we cycled with many people, I fixed a few punctures and chatted away to anyone who would listen, Sanjeev liked a chat, as did Ranjit, Rachael and Zoe were just focused on finishing each day.

The last day, a sixty odd miles to Paris, a lot of the slower pace people had headed out really early not wanting to be last, we got off fairly early as I knew we had a few undulations to contend with. Sandra's leg was gone completely she was dosed up with Ibuprofen and she struggled from the off. I cycled behind her for a while and when we hit a hill you could see she was basically cycling with one leg pushing and pulling. We stopped off for a coffee before lunch and it gave her a needed boost. People started to pass us and we soon became last, some people had obviously been picked up and dropped further down the road in the love bus. There was no way we were getting in that bus; we made it to lunch James came up to me and gestured we had to go, we had only just arrived and now everyone was leaving, it was only ten miles to the holding point so we carried on.

The procession into Paris all together is one of the best things I have ever experienced in my life. The French love a cyclist and toot their horns and cheer you, Skyline stop traffic dead for you and hang out of the windows. It is truly amazing and when you see The Eifel Tower your heart pounds.

Sandra made it, what a special moment. The determination to get through even with an injury like that was inspiring to me, if the Route 66 team had that attitude we wouldn't have a problem at all.

That evening we all had a celebratory meal, it was a nice bunch of people many thanking me for fixing punctures for them on route or giving them a tube. (Never go out without a spare tube or two) Someone even said to us that they didn't want to be last, which I thought was odd because we all cycled in to Paris together, Sandra said she just didn't want to get in the love bus and she hadn't, whereas about twenty probably had. I think we have been together so long we think the same, it doesn't matter how long it takes as long as you achieve what you set out to do, we had set out to cycle from London to Paris and that's what we did, hopefully I could take this forward onto Route 66.

Back in England I was ready to go out with the lads, the speed wouldn't be great but I had some stamina in the legs. I went out with Barry, Danny and Ross and I was determined to put a good effort in. That was the time

I realized we had added two great riders to the team. Them boys left us for dead on the hills, Ross and I were getting blown to bits I was glad when we hit a coffee stop. I threw all I had into that ride and I came up pretty short, some self-doubt immediately setting in. I had trained hard in the gym, cycled to Paris, cut down on drinking, what more could I do apart from give up smoking? That wasn't going to happen at the moment. It was my pace, I had a comfort zone and if I came out of it I would struggle, unfortunately for me, my comfort zone was two or three miles per hour slower than the rest. I could up the pace if the length of the ride was less than two hours any more and I would pay for it later. It looked like the plan was to do two hour stints on Route 66 so I should be ok I would just have to stick to my training plan and go out on my own and not get demoralized.

We had a team of eight all committed to the trip, Mark was on the mend everyone seemed to be getting on with everyone else ok, we still hadn't managed to get out all together but we all planned on doing a London to Brighton ride in September that Skyline were organizing. The plan being to cycle from home to London and then to Brighton. Ticket sales for the ball were sluggish only Danny seemed to be shifting a load. Most of my friends didn't seem that interested judging by the lack of response coming my way. Its hard work raising money for charity, you have to keep at it time and time again. Mark had managed to get a load of free tyres from Continental. I always rode these tyres so that was a result. Barry was in talks with Alan Rochford from Shorter Rochford Cycles about possible kit sponsorship and Alan agreed to supply us with twenty-four shirts. That is what I call very generous and we all thank Alan very much for that.

So at last a few kind companies were helping us out, things were starting to happen. Casey was working at a friend's house. Carmel and Malc's and they offered to hold a garden party for us, there are good people around in this age of selfishness and greed.

I went with Sandra to Kefalonia for a quiet week away, all the work and cycling to Paris had worn me out. Angela and Chris who owned the hotel were pleased to see us, we had been before. We hired bikes and rode every day; I was trying to get a bit of hill work in but not great distances. We would ride in the morning get back to the hotel where Sandra would have a sunbathe and I would sit at the pool bar along with Nick, Bob, Ryan, Chris and Michael and watch the Tour de France, the afternoon sessions seemed to last a long time. Michael the barman was not really into the Tour, but I enjoyed explaining it to him and I hope he enjoyed listening. I recall one night a guy saying to me your on holiday and all you do is watch the TV, it made me chuckle because he had sat by the pool all day, whereas I had cycled forty miles in the morning, anyway what did it have to do with him what I did? He could piss off.

It was a nice break and I felt I had put a bit of hard work in, the legs should be able to get up any climb now.

It was mid June by now and to my utter amazement everyone was still committed to doing the ride. Everyone was getting stuck into there own training programme.

I started to believe for the first time that the target of seven days was achievable.

I must apologize to all the people who work with me at this time, because all I was talking about was Route 66, I would come in on a Monday morning and go on about fundraising, training rides, who was upsetting me, what I needed to do before I went. So to Matt, Katie, Tony, Paul, Joelski, Hattie, Ant and Helen I'm sorry it must have been fairly boring listening to me at tea break every day, in fairness I'm the only one who talks anyway unless I've dragged Casey along to work, he can talk for England too, maybe it's a family trait. I know it would have been boring because I have worked with guys before and the only thing they talk about all day is football, they get up and watch it on Sky news, they go to work and read the paper then moan about what they are reading, then go home or to the pub to watch the big game, obviously there is a big game on every night these days, I suppose it's the same with rugby fans or fishing fanatics, but football being the big sport always takes over the conversation. At least the team who I share the tearoom with have a wide range of interests and were quite happy to let me bang on about the trip and seemed genuinely interested.

Back to training, I went out with Mick who had been putting a lot of work in on the bike. I could see the improvement especially on the hills. He had his new super lightweight carbon bike and was now in cleats. We had a bit of a disaster whilst out, Mick punctured but the tubes we had wouldn't fit, the puncture repair kit we had looked like it was sold back in 1977 and the glue didn't seem to work very well, so we had a twenty miler back to my house stopping every three to four miles to re-inflate his tyre (I don't think his rims were too impressed).

It was great to get out with Mick I always enjoyed cycling with him and I usually wasn't too far off the pace. Mick was so excited about the challenge he had put a huge amount of effort into his own fitness and fundraising, we would be on the phone to each other every other day as we were with Ross, we were living the dream anyone looking in must have thought we were bonkers or just middle age men trying to re-live their youth.

I have a lot of time for Mick and over the last few years we have become good mates. He genuinely likes doing things for charity and always gives a hundred Percent. Sometimes he gets a bit pissed off if people are not pulling their weight and that is fair enough. With Mick, not unlike me, you get what you see even when we both are struggling, we just get on with it and try not to show any weakness. You need people like Mick to keep everyone on their toes, even if he does trample on a few at times; its all done with good intention. You could be sure he would be ready for the trip.

Chapter 11

Day Five – The Road To Santa Fe
(Tetchy Tuesday as I remember it)

This was the day most of us had been looking forward to, the climb to Santa Fe, the town itself is supposed to be very pretty with lots of old brickwork and a bit of history. I certainly had a vision of sitting on a terrace somewhere in the scorching heat sipping on a nice cold larger taking it all in (sometimes I am very naive).

Mick and Andy were on the road; they had set off just after sunrise. We had managed to take a couple of good photos with a beautiful red sky in the background. I was very excitable this morning having grabbed a bit of sleep during the night. It was a very windy day (wasn't it always?) but pleasantly warm, Ross and Mark were grabbing a bit of shuteye whist I was boring Kenny, Steve and Ian. I think Casey was up and about probably eating or looking for food. It was uphill all the way; not very steep but just up, up and up with no let up. We stopped and the boys refuelled, then we headed onto the forty-mile changeover point and parked up. We were in the middle of nowhere with very little traffic around. Ian got the saucepan of water on the stove and then went outside to service and clean the bikes up, King Kenny and Steve got the frying pan out and cooked us up a feast of something, I drank about six coffee's and smoked a few cigars it was a nice break and well needed. Andy and Mick were taking a while, but it must have been a gruelling ride for them, I was hoping our ride would be a bit easier, we couldn't be that far from the top. The old troopers came into sight and looked very pleased to see us, Casey and I were ready to go, we had a quick chat first, Mick was telling us the wind had been ferocious and the climb was a killer. We took it all in then cycled off on the road to Santa Fe.

It wasn't too bad, could this be like yesterday rolling up and down? It certainly seemed that way; a couple of big ups then a nice downhill stretch. We came to a big junction a left hand turn and then the bloody wind in your face. Today was going to prove to be a hard day. We were still rolling up and down, a bit more up than down, but nevertheless the downhill usually gives you a bit of respite, but not today. As we approached the brow of a climb the wind would just drive us back, it was easier climbing than going downhill.

We cracked on and the wind died down for a while, Casey attacked a climb and I let him go he was about fifty yards ahead. The next thing a dog came running out of a driveway and nearly got a chunk of his leg, he was up and out of the saddle and off like a rocket. The dog gave up and ambled back towards the drive entrance, then he spotted me. I stopped and waited for him to go back towards the house thinking I might have a chance to sprint past him, unfortunately the dog was having none of that and stood in the middle of the road growling and almost daring me to come past, it was a stand off. What was I going to do I didn't fancy my chances? As if by magic a car came past tooting it was Sandra and Bernice, they pulled up beside Casey further down the road. I was gesturing them to come back, after a while the penny dropped and they reversed back. I took my chance I rode up alongside them, I was the opposite side to the dog we then sped past him as fast as my legs would take me, the bugger realized what was going on, but we had a bit of speed up and I made my escape. We stopped about a hundred yards up the road and to be honest guys I took five and had a smoke and a chat with the girls. They were going to drive up to the change over and wait for us there. Fully recharged we set off again, low and behold the wind came back with a vengeance and the hills kept a coming.

Casey was getting very frustrated, it was the first time on the trip I had seen him this way. We were doing about eight miles an hour in sections no matter how much effort we put in we just couldn't go any faster. I encouraged him to keep plugging away and we would get there, he has thanked me since a few times and I was glad to help him out for once rather than the other way around.

Well we wanted to climb Santa Fe and it had proved a big test, but as we neared the end of our section we both had a wry smile on our faces, another tale to tell in years to come.

We reached the Winnebago, Ross and Mark had just left, there had been a lot of chat about the length of time it was taking at changeover, so the plan was to try and speed things up by getting the bus ahead to get the bikes off the rack and the riders ready to go, I hadn't realized this included a jump start. The girls were nowhere in sight the crew said they hadn't stayed long, this was a bit odd, I would phone Sandra later, maybe they needed to get to their hotel?

We got the bikes on the rack grabbed a drink and chased the guys down, in fairness they were not far; the wind and climb keeping them at bay as it had with us. We pulled up beside the guys Ross wasn't very happy he shouted in the driver's window, "This is fucking ridiculous it's taken us half an hour to do four and a half miles." No one said anything he and Mark cycled on, the crew informed me that Ross wasn't impressed we were on the Santa Fe climb, I'd forgotten we had changed the plan and maybe I needed a chat with him to make sure he was alright, I got my chance a few miles down the road when we came to a stop to check the route.

Ross was on his bike I just went over and asked if he was ok, "No I'm fucking not actually I'm really pissed off, I made a decision yesterday and when I got up this morning it had been overturned." I was a bit gob smacked to say the least I replied, "It wasn't your decision to make, we are a team of eight, you can't make a decision like that without speaking to everyone else, I spoke to everyone else and we all wanted to do it, so that's why we're doing it." It was a bit tense then he went on his way with Mark. I have known Ross for years and he is one of my best friends, this is the first occasion we have ever had words; well on this scale anyway. Make no mistake this was proving to be a hard trip physically but the mental stress was also taking its toll. The target of seven days was what we were striving for but at what cost? What was the point in pushing ourselves over the edge to save five minutes here or there? The decision to miss out Santa Fe had nearly caused the trip to implode, it was a strange moment. In Ross and Marks defence I'm sure they thought they were doing the right thing, unfortunately the consequences of missing Santa Fe out were too great for the rest of us. (I couldn't have handled the piss take when we returned home for one.) Let's leave it at that and move on, I have not spoken to Ross about it since and it's best left on the road.

The guys hit the top of the climb at about six miles then it was down hill, we never really saw Santa Fe it just whizzed by. Barry later informed me it was a lovely place and the food was great (cheers Bazza).

We got to the change over and it was another jump start; this saving a couple of minutes was getting on my nerves, I know we had wasted a lot of time to date but it didn't seem right. There seemed to be a few private discussions going on which is never healthy, but I was hoping we could all buckle down and get on with the job in hand. Ross and Mark hit the front RV and off they went. We jumped in the back bus with Andy and Mick and caught up with Dan and Barry on the road. After the long day climbing we were making good pace on the down hill and it looked like we would be getting back in the saddle sooner than we thought. Dan and Barry put a good stint in, Dan's flu finally easing off a bit! Andy and Mick were up and ready to go, the night was closing in. We were all feeling a bit tired tonight it had been a long hard day, Casey had caught up with a bit of sleep, and I was mulling the day's events over in my head. Dan and Barry had finished, we had a bit of a chat then they headed off for a sleep. Mick and Andy had a fair bit of Interstate tonight and I didn't envy them at all, a fair bit was down hill but the roads were pretty busy. We would let them go in front, wait for a while then drive past and wait for them at the next junction, make sure they were ok then repeat the process. We had got to the last junction and were waiting for them I think it was a long section about eleven miles. I was making up the water bottles, the only problem was we had no water. The crew phoned the front bus, they would come back and meet us on route, we had a bit of spare time so we set off. We were driving for about ten miles or so then took a right turn, the road we were on can only be described as not fit for bicycle's, it was a stone surface not unlike type one with a dash of concrete every half a mile, I was hoping this wasn't on our stint, apparently it was eight miles long. It was so dark; all sorts of things were running across the alleged road, there was even a massive bull, literally on the road. I'm thinking if you see one bull who knows how many are out there? We met the other bus, took on water, changed drivers and headed back to meet Andy and Mick. Apparently they would be cycling the first mile of the track and we would do the rest, great!!! Andy and Mick were glad to see us, they had had a hard time on the Interstate and were ready for a rest, they took on some food and finished their stint. Mick was well pleased he didn't have to cycle the rest of the track as he got off he gave me a pat on the back and wished me luck on that surface. Casey didn't look like he was going to enjoy this ride either, especially when James came up to us and explained he would have to leave us as they were running on empty; no fuel. They would have to back track to the nearest town, as there was nothing the way we were going. We saddled up and headed out; it was horrendous, pick your line and avoid the potholes, try and stay on the compacted bits, avoid all the mice or rats or whatever they were, keep your eye out at the sides for bulls or coyotes or them skunks, oh it was a very intense seven miles. The one thing I was praying for was to not have a puncture; I really didn't want to be stuck out here trying to change a tube. Miraculously we made it; even the rednecks in the four by fours that occasionally drove past missed us, we paused for a drink and wondered where the bloody hell the van was, it was getting cold so we pushed on, we caught up with the Interstate and travelled along side it for a bit. We would be on one side then go under it and go down a big dip, all of a sudden it would become freezing and I mean really cold you could feel it breathing in. We had cycled about fourteen miles and no sign of anyone perhaps the van had run out of petrol? We were at a junction trying to decide which way to go, a vehicle pulled up behind us and someone got out and walked toward us. He was an old boy looked about ninety. He was the sheriff or local police, his hand itching above his gun holster. He asked us if we were lost and what we were up to? We explained the trip and that our support vehicle was someway back (not wanting to tell him we were looking for orange arrows on his signs) He then told us he had seen it going up and down and stopping and starting, he had wondered what it was up to. That explained it, it was obviously the front vehicle – we were on the right track – he pointed us in the direction it went and we set off, I noticed the orange arrow not ten feet down the road. The van finally caught up with us after seventeen miles what a relief; it had been an interesting night to say the least. We were heading towards Gramps and I was feeling a little tired I was sure to sleep well tonight. The van pulled up beside us they were going to drive ahead to the change over location, the front bus was going to be at a garage a couple of miles away but if it couldn't park there it would be a further three miles down the road. Alas it was a further three miles down the road. We arrived expecting Ross and Mark to have already left, we were somewhat surprised to find them still around. They had all been fast asleep and only awoke about twenty minutes earlier so they were nowhere near ready to leave. It was around midnight, maybe a tad later and for breakfast they were eating pizza not ideal really before a forty-mile ride, but very ideal after a forty-mile ride, washed down with a milky coffee. The crew were certainly looking after Casey and me, he needed food I needed coffee and every time we stopped that's what we got. Ross and Mark headed out, we got our stuff together and jumped in the front bus as it was our turn for a long sleep. We got washed and Casey jumped into bed. I had a chat with Greg, he was looking very tired himself, it had been a tense day for every one, I apologized to him for the teams behaviour and stressed it was the sleep deprivation and fatigue affecting everyone, I gave him a pat on the back and told him what a great job the crew were doing and it would all come out in the wash. He thanked me for that which was nice and

I headed off to join Casey for a sleep. I lay awake for a while thinking what a day, it had been really hard but was that the riding or all the stress? Tetchy Tuesday had drawn to an end and thank God we had made it through, the trip was going by so quickly now we only had about five sessions to go. I was lying there thanking my legs for doing a good job and not letting me down. Barring any incidents we were going to make it to Santa Monica and I fell asleep dreaming of an ice-cold lager on the beach.

Looking confident at the start.

"C'mon Mark it's not the Graveyard shift"

Everyone looking a bit serious here

Ah, team bonding

Photography guru Steve has the camera turned on him at the half way point

"It's just straight Mick for another 1,200 miles"

My Dads a legend

The team time trial specialists Danny, Bazza and Sparrow Legs

The road to Santa Fe

Bazza reckons he had no lead left in his pencil

Casey loves a selfie

Unable to draft up Stigreaves Pass when you're only doing 2mph

Victorville, our last night shift

Santa Monica Pier, this felt so good

King Kenny and Ian, thanks for coffee,
pizza and bike maintenance

I couldn't leave out James and Will, thanks for driving
and cleaning the toilets!!!!!

Chapter 12

Road Trip To Brighton

At last we were all going out on a training ride together apart from Mark who had a big night out booked up and didn't think he could make it the next day.

The events had nearly all passed by now, the most memorable being Bernice's parents afternoon tea party, Jean certainly could make a good cake and had put an enormous effort in, Ross fired up the barbeque and I had smuggled in a few beers, which went down very well.

Casey had finished his degree and decided to work for me up until the trip, as he and his girlfriend Jess were going to travel around America after the trip for a few weeks so he didn't see much point in trying to get a job yet. I was pleased; it was probably going to be the last summer we worked together, he had been working with me in the summers since a very young age so it would be the end of an era.

We had a big team meeting at Ross' house on 4 September to discuss final planning for the Ball. Casey was full of the flu and I was just starting to get it, I never normally got colds or flu but over the next few days I would certainly get this one. The whole team were together and you could feel the excitement, it really was going to happen. Sandra and Bernice had put a big effort into the ball and we had all badgered friends and colleagues to buy tickets. It was looking like we could make some serious money for the charities, this could save the day and make the trip worthwhile.

As with anything you organize you might have different opinions on how to do it. We had a couple of things to discuss, the first being seat covers. Bernice wanted to cover all the seats to make the hall look stunning, I was not against the idea of covering the seats, I just thought it was an unnecessary cost, on the night it did look stunning no doubt about that. I conceded defeat Bernice was not giving in on this one. The next was a champagne reception, we took a vote and it went in favour of the champagne, so again I conceded defeat and we moved on and enjoyed the rest of our night together.

I woke early on the day of our London to Brighton trip, the plan was to meet up with Barry, Dan and Ross at South Mimms service station, about five miles from where I live, Mick and Andy would meet us in London at Clapham Common for the official start. We left home at around 4am and met Dan and Barry. Ross was a bit late; he had a puncture on the way, changing tubes in the middle of the night would prove useful for Route 66. I was riddled with man flu and was concerned as to whether I would make it to London let alone Brighton! The ride into the smoke was stunning; hardly any cars, just the odd clubber on the way home. It was so peaceful.

Riding along the Thames at that time of the morning was well worth the early start. I was struggling for pace as always and my nose was running like a tap, I felt like shit to be honest and thought about throwing in the towel, but I needed the mileage in my legs so decided to give it a go. We met the other guys and I told everyone that my aim today was just to get to Brighton and not to wait for me I'd see them at the finish. We set off and I was soon isolated I couldn't keep the pace. Casey and Andy dropped back and pulled me along to lunch. What a relief to get to lunch; it was a Skyline event so you knew you would be well fed. I bumped into Hans who I had met cycling to Paris it was great to see him, that old boy was an inspiration to anyone who knew him. I phoned Sandra and put Hans on the phone, they had a chat as they had got on well on the trip. I perked right up, this guy had beaten cancer I just had to beat a poxy cold.

It was just Casey me and Ross now, the others having left as the plan was they were going to cycle back and put one hundred and fifty miles in. We were meeting Sandra and Bex and they were going to drive us back. The cycling back had been a bit of an issue, Mick was quoted as saying, "If you can't cycle 150 miles in a day how are you going to cycle Route 66?" Casey normally easy going had been incensed with this statement. He had said to me, "Dad were not cycling 150 miles a day, its only about 90 and Mick hasn't got to go out and work for eight hours in the cold tomorrow." I knew where he was coming from, he had helped me with my training programme and I was feeling fit apart from the flu so we had decided to just do the eighty-odd miles today.

We set off with Ross and I felt much better (must have been the coffee). I was looking forward to the climb up Ditchling Beacon. Ross was cramping up pretty bad, we had to make a few stops, it was unusual for Ross as he was normally very strong and I would usually only see him at the finish of an event. We were a team and like Andy had stayed with me we stayed with Ross. We hit the Beacon and Casey rode off to challenge himself, the plan was to all attack it and re-group at the top. I managed it just about, sucking in big air at the top, we then waited for Ross. We had a break and headed down the other side toward Brighton, I stopped to put my rain jacket on with Casey. Ross had a new lease of life and flew past the next time we saw him was at the finish. Sally from Skyline was at the finish and as always seemed pleased to see us; we were always pleased to see her especially at the finish of a trip! Sandra and Bex had not faired so well, these days' cars and vans don't come with a spare wheel you get a puncture kit. I had asked the salesman when I bought the van about a spare wheel and what good is a puncture kit if you shred a tyre, his answer had been when do you ever shred a tyre these days. Sandra had today and had to wait for the AA who took her to get a tyre, lucky it was not Sunday night or else we would have been getting the train back. The girls eventually arrived and found us in a pub waiting to order Sunday lunch, we had been discussing the fact that the guys had probably cycled home by now, little did we know.

The next day at work we dissected the ride. I was totally happy with my performance, if I could keep going feeling that bad, I should be ok on Route 66.

My legs didn't ache at all; the gym sessions must have done me the world of good. Casey staying with me had ridden well with in himself, he wanted to ride Route 66 with me and I was relishing the thought of being with my son on the trip. Mick and the others hadn't got on so well on the way home, they hit a big thunder-storm and decided to abandon cycling home and got on the train. Casey remarked, "Will Mick not be able to ride Route 66 because he couldn't cycle 150 miles in a day?" It was light hearted banter but it did make me chuckle.

I had lost a fair bit of weight over the course of eight months and felt quite toned. Andy had lost an absolute shed load of weight, whereas Mick had lost a bit but seemed to be stronger than Andy on the hills, which was a big surprise. Ross had lost an awful lot of weight in a very short time and was looking really good. Casey studied nutrition as part of his degree and he doesn't say much to other people but to me he expressed a concern about the amount of weight some of the guys were losing. If you're training for an endurance event you can't lose that much weight that quickly, especially if you're on a diet of shake supplements rather than food. I was doing exactly what he told me and that was to eat more and train more, which I had been and I was still losing weight!

It was 9 September, less than a month to go, every time I went to bed my mind was in a spin, had I trained enough, could I actually do this, did I really want to do this? All these questions would be answered in about a month's time.

The next day Mick sent an email out to everyone, the one thing that sticks in my mind was and I quote, "Personally eight hours ride time a day is not enough, that will give me 16 hours downtime and boredom will set in." I was worrying whether I could actually finish Route 66 and here was Mick looking like he wanted to cycle it all, if all the other guys were thinking the same I would be in serious trouble, eight hours a day in the saddle would be more than enough for me.

We had the Ball coming up and everyone was focused on that at the moment, ticket sales had gone fairly well, I hadn't sold as many as I thought I might but I wasn't going to let it get me down I was going to enjoy the evening. After the band I was going to do a DJ set, which I had worked hard on, I knew the younger people coming were looking forward to a bit of a disco, Ross had said to save bringing my gear the band were going to let us run it through their P.A. which was perfect I had also written a song for the trip which I was planning on performing, but I wasn't going to tell anyone about it I was just going to do it on the night, I was hoping the lads would appreciate it.

Along with Ross, Mick and Andy our nigh on two year journey would be over soon, I can't speak for the others but for me getting this far had been a miracle, I had been through times when I thought it really wouldn't happen. Riders had been in and out, friendships tested to breaking point, I knew the real challenge lay ahead but I was totally unaware of how tough it would really be.

Chapter 13

Day Six – Petrified Forest,
The Interstate and Shall We Just Give Up

I woke early, I got up expecting to be at a garage but when I opened the door of the RV all I could see was an entrance sign to Petrified Forest. I looked around, the interstate was fifty yards away and we were in a car park with one other vehicle, which soon moved off, and left a pile of rubbish, even in the states you get litterlouts. Ian got up and made us a cup of coffee while I tried to unblock the toilet I had just used. Everyone else was sound asleep we went for a stroll and discussed the fact that I, along with Casey would be cycling along the interstate as no other roads seemed to be around. For once the wind was not in your face it was sort of behind to one side. Over the course of the next two hours or so while we waited for Mick and Andy the wind would come full on from the side and slightly in front, lucky that would push us away from the traffic. Weather warnings were being issued of strong gusts warning vehicles to be careful. I had a nice chat with Ian for an hour or so before anyone else stirred, we then got the call the guys were only an hour away. Breakfast got under way and the other bus soon came trundling down the road to meet us. Everyone was up and about and in good spirits, I was so relieved as yesterday had been a struggle for everyone. We took a few photos including a tour favourite of mine with Barry looking petrified (I would soon be looking like that!). Andy and Mick seemed to be taking a while, the reason being they had stopped to repair a puncture, we were waiting for them by the ramp of the Interstate. We were getting told to get on our way but I was having none of it. They came into view about a mile up the road. Ross was insistent that we got going but I wanted to talk to them about conditions and any tips they might have, they had done a fair bit of the interstate over the last few days where as me and Casey in comparison had been a bit more lucky. They arrived and told us to watch ourselves the lorries were moving pretty fast and you got sucked all over the place. We tentatively headed down the ramp, crikey chaps this wasn't good. It was a good job the wind was blowing us away from the traffic or else we would have been under a wheel. The interstate signs were flashing wind warnings; we had about twelve miles of this to contend with.

We followed the plan; come up at every junction to avoid crossing traffic lanes then re-join. I was trying to keep Casey on my right away from the traffic, he was moaning that I was to near the traffic; we both were worrying a bit. To make it worse we were heading into road works the hard shoulder we were on now being used as the inside lane. We took a decision to cross the traffic and ride in the shut lane at this point the RV pulled in and told us to get in, we said no and carried on. I don't know what the workman laying tarmac thought of us cycling past, I didn't really care it was safer than the inside lane.

The road works came to an end and we approached the junction we were to come off at. Greg was at the junction to tell us the route we were to take was shut so it was back on the interstate for a further few miles probably to Holbrook.

The wind was tough and it had shifted; it was now hitting us still from the left but more of a head wind. As if by magic King Kenny come up beside us, he didn't care about minimum speed limits he was going to protect us for as long as he could we were so relived although the gusts were rocking the RV about. At last the wind eased and Kenny pulled away, our last couple of miles seemed a bit easier.

We left the interstate and saw the RV at a garage on the other side of the road I thought I saw Sandra and Bernice but we plowed on. A couple of miles later Sandra and Bernice pulled up beside us and we took a short breather, they had past us on the interstate and were quite concerned we were in the closed lane. We headed off and stopped a couple of times for photos it was a nice town, plenty to see. The interstate didn't seem too bad now we had ridden the storm. We had about three or four miles to go when we saw the RV. We stopped to see what was happening. Kenny explained the next bit on the interstate was about nine miles so the change over was going to be now. Ross and Mark were ready to go, Kenny explaining the plan, as he had to us. Dan and Barry were singing our praises, Barry was concerned I was close to the traffic; I told him I was being a protective father thinking the Lorries would hit me not Casey. That stint took a lot out of me physically and mentally but I seemed to be getting stronger day by day, there was life in the old dog yet. Speaking of dogs only two more night shifts then the dogs would be a distant memory, could we make it through unscathed?

Our bikes were loaded it was time to move on, we drove about twenty yards when the phone went, it was Ross and Mark they were heading back. We waited a couple of minutes then they appeared, they explained to Kenny they felt the wind was too strong, Kenny was stressing from a Skyline point of view, he couldn't see any health and safety issues but it was entirely up to them. They loaded the bikes in the RV with us and we drove about eighteen miles to where Route 66 split with the interstate, it was a long very quiet eighteen miles no one really said much, we stopped let them out and they went on their way again. At first I felt a bit cheated after having ridden with Casey in such conditions, I would certainly not have let Casey ride if I thought it had been too dangerous, it was all dangerous really; anytime you get on a bike its dangerous. You have to look at things subjectively though and if they were worrying about riding that section then it was probably best they didn't ride it.

We needed to get some supplies and I wanted to eat so badly, we found a supermarket and me, Barry, Dan and Casey hit a McDonalds, we had two large meals each and felt so much better for it. For once Casey didn't need to tell me to eat, I knew I needed food. We got back on the road and I tried to have a shower but we ran out of water, I spent ages with bottles of water and wet wipes, oh the allure of a road trip.

We kept having a lot of chat about speeding up the change overs, I was getting pissed off now and I must thank James for calming me down. I could see why they wanted to change things, we were running behind but I hadn't signed up to do jump starts, why didn't we just drop riders off down the road and have everyone riding at the same time because that is what it seemed like we were being asked to do. I phoned Sandra and told her I might ride the last few hundred miles with Casey and they could jump start as much as they liked. I suppose I may have been tired and not looking at the whole picture I just felt decisions were being made out of my control and I didn't like it. Maybe I'm too opinionated you draw your own conclusions I just wanted to do what I thought was right.

Ross and Mark swapped with Dan and Barry then we headed to an RV park to dump the toilet and take on some water. You could get a shower for £5 dollars and the guys made the most of it, pity they didn't wash and dry cycling shorts that is what we all craved for. We were somewhere near Flagstaff which is the highest point on the trip. The radio was forecasting snow at 2am could we make it through and be on our way downhill? I was hoping so. Barry and Dan took us out the other side of Flagstaff and we met with the others. Mick and Andy took over, all I can remember was seeing signs warning of bears. I started to get my gear together, Andy and Mick had more Interstate; they were definitely getting a fair share of Interstate, it was bad enough in the day but at night it was awful, the only good thing it looked like we had missed the snow. The crew informed me that we didn't have any Interstate tonight so to say I was pleased was an understatement. We had just past a town called Seligman, again it would be nice to go back to these places and stay a while we really did not see them at all. Tonight we would travel through Peach Springs and finish near Thruxton. The trouble was at night you didn't stop to take a photo as you had to stay pretty tight with the riders on the road if you were in the RV and if you were on the bike you wouldn't want to stop to long because you couldn't see what was around you. We swapped over and it was great, we were heading downhill the wind was sideways and not so in front we could get the miles in tonight, it was bloody freezing though. All of a sudden it started to rain, we flew after the RV and flagged it down, our clothes already wet we should have changed everything but were running out of gear anyway. Well it pissed down for about two hours I have never seen rain like it, it was horizontal we had the opportunity to go really fast and I was shouting at Casey to slow down as we were riding at an angle of about 45 degrees. Steve pulled up beside and told us to get in, Casey was having none of it telling me this was the first bit of downhill we had and we were carrying on. We started singing "Bob" by NOFX, ha ha, then moved on to dance music, we were laughing our heads off if we rode through it everyone else would have to. It bloody stopped about an hour before we finished, I couldn't feel my feet or my hands, my hands were stuck in the position of my gear levers. We got on board, stripped off and jumped in the shower, it was a drizzle but it was hot. I put some tracksuit bottoms on and made some jam on toast followed by jam on toast and more jam on toast, washed down with milky coffee, we were so happy another stint done. I got my head down. My mind was ticking away but I managed to get some sleep. Ross and Mark were on the road, I must have slept through most of their stint and the changeover, when I awoke, Danny, Bazza and Greg were on the road they were lost and waiting for us, they were cold and wet and needed a change of clothes. Greg had wanted to ride the big climb coming up at Stigreaves Pass that is why he was on the road. He probably needed to get out of the RV for a couple of hours. Bazza and Danny were trying to find dry clothes, any clothes would do at this stage of the game, Danny was doing the sniff test on his gear to find out what wasn't quite as stinky and could be worn another day. It was the early morning on Thursday our last 24 hours were about to start. I felt good everyone was still in one piece, the mood had at last got back to where it should be, yes today would be an epic day a day to savour, let's get the job done.

Chapter 14

The Ball

The day of the ball had arrived, it was going to be a long day and hopefully we would raise some serious money.

Sandra, Bernice, Ross and I arrived at Sopwell House about mid-day, we had many things to get sorted, Ross had made some banners, we had bunting, raffle prizes, auction items, table plans and projectors to set up. Ross, Bernice and Sandra had put a massive effort in to get everything just right. I was just assisting; a bit of a spare part. The order of events was all sorted, jobs had been allocated, Ross and Mick were to talk, Dan and Casey would do the heads and tails, I was doing the disco and we were all to collect raffle money. We left about three due to return at five. It was bedlam at our house with people getting ready, we made haste and returned to Sopwell. The band was all set, we finished off a few jobs and we were ready. We had a signed Bradley Wiggins yellow jersey for our star auction prize and Phil Liggett the voice of cycling from television had agreed to auction it off for us. We had a Laura Trott signed top as well and loads and loads of other stuff; people had been so generous.

The place filled up fast and everyone was tucking into the champagne and wine, this could be a good night. Carol from The Willow Foundation had lost her voice a bit and asked me to do a talk for them, I felt honoured. She would read a letter out from a recipient of a special day after I had talked about the charity. We had a guy from Help for Heroes who gave us an interesting talk on how he had been injured and his rehabilitation. The auction went well as did the raffle, on the night we raised about £12,000 – unbelievable really – we were only expecting about £6,000.

I would like to thank my children Becky and Casey who managed to fill a table each. So to Georgia, Hannah, Jess, Rhian and their partners thank you girls. Casey had Sam, Emma, Barney, James, Jess, Emma and Emily. I myself had Anne and Grahame, Emma and Fraser, Demetri, Chris and Sue, Ants and Robbie, Tracy and Tom, Theresa and of course Gezza although he wasn't doing the ride anymore he still came out and supported us.

I felt it was a poor effort on my behalf, either I hadn't tried hard enough to get friends to attend or I just haven't got many friends, I decided not to ponder too much on that one.

I would sincerely like to apologise to all the younger people who were led to believe that a disco would follow the band, everything ran late and as much as I tried I was not allowed to play.

So the ball had been a great success, on the surface everything looked on track. In the background Andy had upset some of the others, it had been lingering on for a couple of weeks, me being me, I approached him late on at the ball, hindsight is a wonderful thing but it had not really been the appropriate time. The next day a few phone calls ensued and Ross stepped in and sorted it out. I'm very glad it was ironed out and we could all head to Chicago in good form.

As I write my story some team members have been trying to get me to leave any disagreements we had out of this book, I have thought long and hard about this and concluded the story should be told how it happened. It would be a very short book if it went: "We had no trouble raising the money, we all got on extremely well and it was easy to ride Route 66"

I don't think so, that wasn't how it happened, it was bloody hard work from start to finish and as a team we all performed well and did what we could do under extreme conditions or what seemed extreme to us at the time.

With the ball out of the way it was all about the ride, we were about to take on the mother road. Casey and I discussed what we needed and what we could double-up on. The thing with cycling in America was that if we forgot anything I was sure we could buy it out there.

Chapter 15

Day 7 – The Dessert,
Coyotes and Santa Monica

It was the early hours of Thursday morning, we had just rendezvoused with Danny, Bazza and Greg, they were soaking wet and needed to change. They had been a bit lost and had waited for us to catch up. We had left Kingman behind and were now heading towards Cool Springs; the plan was to enjoy the morning and have a bit of fun.

We pulled up at Cool Springs and took a look around the gift shop we all seemed to buy a few items this morning. Danny Greg and Bazza arrived on their bikes and had a break. For once no one was rushing. Casey wanted to join the boys to take on Stigreaves Pass so he got his kit on, Will also wanted a go so I lent him my bike, shoes and top, he passed on the offer of my shorts though! Mick, Andy and I passed up the opportunity knowing we still had another 80 miles each to do. I do regret this decision, as it wasn't as long as I thought it would be, I might have made it.

Steve got his camera out and took a few shots. It's a good job Steve was on the trip he took 700 photos and has left us with a lasting memory. Kenny was also with us and enjoying the break it had been a hard six days.

We followed the boys up the pass shouting abuse as we passed each rider – or should I have said shouted encouragement? Ross, Mark, James and Ian were at the top of the pass with the other RV, it was a good coming together of all the riders and crew.

I was full of energy today bouncing around all over the place, I knew we had it in the bag, timing wasn't important, just finishing would be a miracle after my first ride into the wind almost seven days ago. We followed the boys downhill I was wishing I was on the bike, Kenny was driving and we were flying down the hill into Oatman, I kept looking at Mick as we rounded corners at what seemed a very sharp pace. Oatman seemed like another place you would want to stop at and have a look around, but alas we had to crack on to get ready for Mick and Andy to take over. The old warhorses were a bit tired; I got the impression they were looking forward to seeing the ocean. This morning's rides should be ok it would soon get flatter as we approached needles and the Mohave dessert and if that wind could just be kind to us. Casey was asleep in the back bed along with Barry; Dan was also getting his head down so I thought I might do the same. I laid down pondering on things for a while and then fell asleep, the next thing Kenny was shouting at me to get ready. I gave Casey a few calls before he emerged, we pulled up and the crew got the bikes ready. I must have had a good sleep; it was the first time on the trip I had to rush to get ready. Kenny was telling us to get going as they were just over the hill and I couldn't be bothered to argue so we headed off. Mick and Andy had been on the road for about four hours that was a long time they must have had a tough section. I later found out from Mick that he had really struggled and found it one of his hardest sessions.

It was a lovely day, nice scenery not too much wind and not too much traffic. Andy and Mick had ridden us into California – our last state. We hit a section of road that just seemed to be straight for miles and miles, if a car did go past it was in view for about twenty minutes. Along the side of the road people had arranged rocks into messages to loved ones. These messages also went on for miles; we stopped for a drink watching out for spiders and snakes. I was annoyed with myself for not waiting for Andy and Mick, so I decided I would have a cigar to put us back to where we should have been, I felt a lot better for it to.

It was about twenty-five miles without a turn, had the Romans been here? We started to climb and rounded a corner, a descent followed and we thought we could see a spot were the RV would be, if it wasn't it might be another ten miles along a straight road. It had been another good ride, under three hours, I was pleased with that. It was now our turn to join the front bus and a chance to get our heads down, or more importantly get a shower at an RV park. We probably stopped for another burger and shake; it's a bit of a blur now so many burgers and shakes. I do remember stopping for a shower that was fantastic, simple things like a proper shower and clean clothes and a shave!

The rest of the day was good we were all getting excited now. It was looking like we would finish within the seven days; most of us would rather have finished about three hours later, who would be around at about 6.30am? Never the less we couldn't stop for a rest because of that. It was about sixty miles to go to where we would rest up and wait for the other RV, I felt tired and thought perhaps it was time for a kip. James was driving and along with Casey I was rocked gently asleep. It seemed to be a bloody long sixty miles, I was bouncing off the bed nearly hitting the ceiling, when I woke all sorts of pandemonium was going on.

Casey was up before me – that was a first, the other RV was currently stuck in the middle of a road someway back and we had doubled back to help them out. It had all been happening when we reached the other RV. It was dark now and the dessert can be a lonely place in the dark. Dan and Barry had punctured about ten miles back from the RV, as they tried to fix it a coyote had walked into the road in front of them and started to howl.

A load more Coyotes approached and started to howl, the guys phoned the police who I think said they could send a sheriff. They then phoned the RV who tried to turn around, taking its rear wheels off the tarmac and into the sand. Two riders were dispatched to help Danny and Barry. It all got sorted Danny and Barry made their escape, a friendly American pulled the RV out and we arrived. We hadn't factored in coyotes in our pre-planning but we will know next time. The guys were a bit shaken up, apparently they don't normally attack people but we were unaware of that at the time. At least we were still all in one piece; what else would pop up in the final hours, surely that was it?

We all took time out at a garage down the road to discuss the remaining mileage; time had slipped away somewhat so it was looking like a later finish. It was time to crack on. Andy and Mick were up again then Casey and I would ride our last shift together. We headed up the road in the front RV and waited in a place that was not the most picturesque. A couple of guard dogs were in a building beside us and I was glad they couldn't get out. Sleep was done for the night, the excitement in the dessert putting paid to that. Andy and Mick arrived they looked relived knowing that was it for them, they would jump in the front RV now and head to the point 20 miles from the finish, have a rest, a wash and be fresh for the last bit of cycling that we would all complete together. Casey and I saddled up and headed off it was going to be one of those nights, a night of dogs barking and giving chase. We hadn't been out long but we soon realised it was going to be a long night. We were heading toward a set of traffic lights when a massive dog came flying out; it was on a chain, but it broke the chain, we were out of our saddles giving it everything we had. The lights were red but we kept going, a huge lorry was coming across our route but we had to keep going, we just made it and the dog was cut off. Bloody hell that was close, we went past a quarry and toward a town where the RV was waiting for us. The crew were in contact with the front RV, we were having trouble finding the route and we would have to back track. We cycled back past the quarry, I could see that dog up ahead, I wasn't going anywhere near it. The RV turned round again it was ok, we were going the wrong way so we would not have to pass the dog.

We finally got on track and continued on our way, the finish line only a hundred and twenty odd miles away. Some towns loved Historic Route 66 others didn't, Victorville certainly did. It was around midnight most people were tucked up in bed, a few stragglers were roaming the streets – you could call them hoodies – and others were just looking through bins for food. It is a strange place at times America; you have vast wealth and extreme poverty living side by side. We have it here, but I do feel we are a bit more compassionate, a lot more charities or it would seem that way.

The road we were going to take was shut; the interstate was six lanes wide each side and no cycles allowed we were stumped. We had to drive a section on the interstate as we could find no alternative. It was a bit disappointing but hey ho; out of our control. We emerged back on the bikes and continued as we rode through a built-up hilly section, we managed to get some good pace and no dog would ever have caught us. We had a great section on the outskirts of The San Bernardino National Forest. We finally finished at Verdemont and Mark and Ross were ready to go. It was odd Casey and I had completed the last ride that we would do on our own, the next ride would be the whole team. Ross and Mark had 32 miles, as did Dan and Barry and then a twenty-mile finish together. It was quite a boring ride through the suburbs of L.A. you had a few houses followed by loads of food outlets, obviously the odd garage then a shopping mall, repeated a hundred times. It was a long ride on weary legs only still driving on with the thought of the imminent finish line. Mick and Andy were up ahead having had a good night's rest and were raring to go. Mileage had gone a bit pear shaped, we would now only have to cycle ten together, judging by the traffic this morning even that might take some time. Sandra was ringing me asking for an E.T.A. it was hard trying to put a handle on how long it would take, I would just keep updating her.

We pulled up to where the other RV was waiting. Andy, Mick and the crew looking very fresh having all showered. One last turn on the bike and we would be on Santa Monica Pier.

Chicago seemed a distant memory, we had seen so much since we started. On a personal note Casey and I had ridden through all kinds of conditions. I had struggled on the first 20 miles the pace was too fast, on our first 40-mile stint we had to battle with the wind, on the first night session getting lost and falling off my bike. Day two saw us getting soaked in the day then an upward 45-miler in the evening. Day three the windy ride to Tulsa and dog attacks at night. Day four, a great day in Texas with Casey jumping in with Danny and Bazza followed by a windy cold night ending in Tucumcari. Day five, the climb to Santa Fe and the evening trip along the dirt track. Day six, Petrified Forest and the Interstate, then the rain chasing us all night as we rode downhill from Flagstaff. Day seven, Casey riding up the pass, then we took on the dessert. At night, more dogs and the town of Victorville.

That's enough reminiscing we still had ten miles to go, we all got on our bikes and we were off. As we cycled together the mood was ecstatic, the team had nearly made it. The riders rode, the crew now took pictures and bossed the traffic around us. You couldn't take it all in really you just wanted to get to the finish. When you cycle in convoy people do tend to take notice of you, especially when your crew is making such a noise. One of the RV's headed off in front, we rode down to Santa Monica Pier with one RV tooting its horn in front of us, our family and friends who could make it were ready and waiting, Champagne at the ready and a cigar. I phoned my daughter she was happy for us, someone was telling me to put the phone down for a photo, I continued on the phone, hence the finish line photo had me talking to my daughter.

Well that was that, we had ridden Route 66, the trip back to the hotel would be our last time in the RV. We got back in and the crew played *We Are The Champions*, what's all that about I hate that song, lucky for me James banged on a bit of *Wu Tang* then we had a bit of *Storm Queen MK* mix, well Casey and I enjoyed it.

We arrived at the Hotel, The Palomar on Wiltshire Avenue it looked like a palace to me. One last job empty all our shit off the RV's, try and get all the stickers off the paintwork then get to the room. Or alternatively meet everyone in the bar, the latter was more appealing and got my vote. We savoured a beer or two or three. All the squabbles and fatigue vanished into the first pint. We were a team and as a team we had reached our goal, we had taken seven days three hours and forty-five minutes to complete our challenge, it felt incredible to me that we actually made it and the only casualty of the trip being Marks bike. I still hadn't taken it all in and I wouldn't until the next day after I had time to reflect in the morning. Tonight was going to be all about the celebration Supper, as I looked around most people had disappeared, it was time to go and savour a shower and get some clean clobber on, I was fortunate to have left my case with Sandra so there would be no musty RV smell on me tonight.

Chapter 16

The Last Supper

We all met in the bar; having been one of the last to leave earlier I was somewhat surprised to be back so soon. Twenty-four of us would wind our way down to the restaurant, this consisted of the eight riders, six crew, Sandra and Bernice, Casey's girlfriend Jess, a couple of Ross's mates, Marks girlfriend, and Barry's father-in-law, sister-in-law and her husband and son. To say the drink was flowing freely was an understatement. The place was ok you could get a steak, that was the main thing. I think a proper steak house would have been better, but it was ok.

Ross and Greg had decided to hold a rugby style Kangaroo court; it involved a fair amount of tequila. King Kenny had done a bunk and a few of the party really didn't want to partake in the tequila. Ross ran through a few things then people started drifting away. It was a celebration meal but everyone was bloody knackered.

So who was left, Greg, Ian, Ross, Bernice, Sandra and I, some were looking a bit worse for wear, I was having a smoke outside and Ian decided he was going back to the hotel the only thing was he headed the wrong way, I went after him and bought him back, the lack of sleep and food had caught up with him. We all headed off from the restaurant it was a long walk back, Greg, Ross and Bernice were all over the place. I don't know what it was but I felt quite sober, I was just dog-tired really. We got back to the hotel in one piece – which was another surprise – we headed to bed others hit the bar; they would regret that in the morning. After the trip the meal seemed a bit of an anti-climax perhaps we should have had a day off then the celebration dinner, maybe we shouldn't have had the afternoon session that always knocks everyone out.

The crew departed early next morning leaving only Greg. The challenge over we would all go our separate ways over the next couple of days, we would grab another meal together before we departed and it gave us all a good laugh, especially if you had the ravioli. I'm saying no more than that.

Chapter 17

In Conclusion

I can honestly say I had the time of my life on this trip. If someone had said to me three to four years ago I would be taking part in a trip like this I would have laughed. I'm not a great sportsman and never have been, training doesn't really come natural to me. I am not a disciplined person (well apart from getting up to go to work) so why take part in something like this? I really don't know, it just seemed like a good idea after London to Paris. I suppose, as you get older you have to look at where you want to be in ten, twenty years time. Do you want to drink and smoke more, maybe sit and watch television or spend all your money going to watch sport? Nothing wrong with those choices at all, I just wanted to lose a bit of weight and try something different. My mate Gooey once said to me after a rugby match, "you're a long time not playing" and he is right (although I played yesterday and I am suffering writing today).

I don't think I will ever top what we did on Route 66, I'm not about to go and walk the North and South pole or go trekking up Kilimanjaro. That's it for me, apart from the fact I'm hoping to ride to Paris with my daughter next year, then I will have cycled with all my family.

I thank my family for putting up with me; I don't usually spend so much time thinking about myself and certainly wouldn't normally spend so much money on a trip. To have my son ride alongside me was every fathers dream, I thank Casey because I honestly believe without him I would not have made it. He kept me strong and focused right from day one. I know some days he was itching to get his head down and ride but he never left me, I like to think I have always taught him to look out for the underdog and he certainly did on this occasion.

What about my teammates? What can I say, everyone gave everything they had and you can't ask for more than that. We all react differently under extreme conditions and we all did.

Endurance is a major factor on a seven-day trip like this. I would say the four guys who worked manually had an advantage on those who worked behind a desk. If you work your body five days a week and always have and still train on top of that, you have to have more endurance than those who only train a couple of nights and ride at the weekend, Your body is just used to seeing it through. If you came home from a non-manual job and specifically trained every night, the balance would tip the other way because you wouldn't be training tired and could work the right muscle groups. Let's face it none of us would do that so that's why it panned out the way it did.

Nutrition also played a massive part both on the trip and before we left. You can't just stop eating and expect it not to affect your performance; some of us didn't eat enough on the trip and some before we left.

I was lucky in having Casey he made me eat much more than I usually do and it paid off for me.

I did not spend enough time riding hard in the saddle before the trip, my problem being I get a bit bored and am not as competitive as the others, but again in hindsight I struggled in the wind and more cycling beforehand would have helped.

I have been asked on numerous occasions what were the highlights of the trip, I don't know about highlights but here are some of my memorable moments,

1. James cutting his finger emptying the toilet, he wasn't happy and needed nurse Kevee to administer some antiseptic cream.
2. Mick's quote, "Well Skyline can fuck off," after being asked to extend his ride again after already extending it.
3. Paying $28 each for what looked like a can of ravioli split between four.
4. Kenny reversing into a signpost and wrecking Mark's bike.
5. Mick's quote before we left, "If you can't cycle 150 miles now how are you going to do it on Route 66," then having to get a train home because it was raining.
6. Andy cycling the whole trip with a bag that nothing ever went in or came out of!
7. Ross and Mark's constant moaning about the graveyard shift, which they choose themselves.
8. Ian not eating or sleeping all week and then wondering why he was pissed on about two pints.

9. Danny Boy making love to a foam roller on a garage forecourt (you had to be there).

10. Steve not happy with the road, deciding to put the back wheels of the Winnebago in the Mohave dessert.

11. Kenny telling Ross and Mark, "From a Skyline point of view I can't see any health and safety issues".

12. Will beating his brother Greg up Stigreaves Pass.

13. Barry and Casey having their little chats in the double bed at the back of the RV, I think they call it male bonding.

14. Me still thinking after seven days that I would beat Casey up a hill.

15. Mick's quote, "Personally eight hours ride time a day is not enough, that will give me 16 hours downtime and boredom will set in". I don't think boredom set in and eight hours a day was plenty.

16. But most of all, fourteen of us still talking after a week together in the RV'S from hell.

I hope you have enjoyed the book. I had so much to put in but didn't want to bore you with a mile-by-mile blow of every dip and turn. I wanted to give you a feel of what it was like being on the road and in the RV and a beautifully descriptive account of blades of grass gently caressing the early autumnal winds as we gently glided by on a cushion of compressed air drenched in rubber would not really be me. It was hard, the RV stunk like shit and friendships were tested, as sleep deprivation and exhaustion set in.

To my fellow riders starting with Casey, well done son, you did yourself proud and helped me out more than you will ever know. Mark, you came on the trip after an operation and had to confront your fear of dogs, not forgetting having to ride someone else's bike, well done fella. Andy you pounded away as always in the big gear and put up with the mess, something that I think must have been difficult for such an organised person. Danny how you managed with the flu is beyond belief; you never let the side down. Baz the engine, you pulled us round and the constant jokes kept my mood up for sure. Mick the warhorse never faulted just ground it out day-after-day. Ross the idea man, you envisaged the trip and without the idea none of us would be here, we all thank you for that.

The crew, Greg, Will, Ian, Kenny, Steve and James it would not have been the same without you guys you really put the work in. Skyline, especially Sally did us proud because without the right crew we would still be stuck out in the dessert somewhere so thanks.

"You don't have to be the best, you have to be the best you can."

Kevee

Chapter 18

Kevees' Blogs

My blogs offer a different take on the challenge; I tried to write one a week from January 2013 until we departed. It gives you a better idea of who was actually putting the time and effort in. Reading back through them it seems Mick did a fair bit of the work, some of his events did really well, others not so well but he never wavered. I mention we were going out to do training rides but most of them didn't happen. I give the other team members a bit of stick, it was all well intended and taken in good spirits. I like to think the blogs were quite amusing but you can be the judge of that.

4/3/13

Well here we go the Route 66 weekly blog. It's been a long time coming; in fact we talked about blogs since Ross first came up with the idea of riding the iconic Route 66. That was at our first meeting back in November 2011. Eight of us attended that meeting, sadly only four of us from the original eight remain. We have had other riders come and go since then but we are now a settled committed team.

Has it been easy to get this far? Life is full of challenges and this has definitely been one. What with personnel changes, choosing the charities, organising fund raising events, sorting out merchandise and jostling juggling work, family life and training it's pretty full on. The best move we have made has proved to be getting Skyline Events to sort out the logistics, thanks Skyline. Having said all that things have come together and the team is not only looking forward to completing the challenge but raising as much money as we possibly can for Willow's and Help for Heroes.

We have all started to train in earnest now and for me, I have put myself on a very tough schedule. It's fair to say I am probably the slowest rider in the team at the moment, I am putting myself through a lot of interval training to try and improve on this and it seems to be paying off. When I have cycled with the guys before on trips I usually struggle the first couple of days, but come good on day three and four, so with this in mind if I train I should be able to pull my weight from the start.

News this week

Our farewell ball will be on 21of September in Saint Albans, details will be on the events page of our website.

Mark, Casey, Daniel and Kevee will be attending a fitness seminar held by Willow's at the Arsenal training ground this week.

Ross is leading a cycle to Cambridge next weekend.

I think that is enough this week I don't want to bore you all on my first blog.

Catch you next week

Kevee

10/3/13

Only 29 weeks before we go, I can't wait now. Daniel and I attended a top tips seminar on Thursday hosted by The Willow Foundation. Speakers included Gary Lewin, England football teams head physio, Jonathon O'Neil former team GB cycling soigneur and a recipient of a Willow special day, whose name I did not get, sorry. He was a very courageous young man suffering from cystic fibrosis, he told us of his daily grind of three hours of physio and how he wished for a day off a week but unfortunately his condition did not allow it. Willow's had provided him with a fantastic day and memory which he cherished. A very enjoyable and informative evening. it seems our winter gym training should pay off and that's coming from the expert's.

Mick has been busy organising a comedy night to be held at The Waterman Arms, Eton on 3 May details will be on here shortly.

Sandra and Bernice have been busy with the Ball organisation, it looks like this will be a sell out so you better get in quick, more details will be up soon.

Ross, Mick, Andy and Mark are due to ride the Wiggle "no excuse" ride next Saturday so if you're on it go and have a chat with the boys.

The Willow bike ride is on 21 July this year. Last year Mick and I had a good day out on this one so get yourself on board details are on their website.

Other news this week Mick has got himself a new bike. He's only gone and got a Planet X, which has caused a bit of bike envy amongst some of the rider's. We are all looking forward to seeing how he gets on in his cleats and on that saddle. An update will be available next Sunday. I went to the gym with Ross yesterday for a bit of circuits and spinning hence that is why I'm sitting here writing the blog; our instructor Kat is trying to kill us I'm sure of it.

Cheers
Kevee

15/3/13
Early blog this week as its St. Patrick's Day on Sunday and I may be unavailable for comment, plus it is the last day of the Six Nations so looks like a good weekend (depending on who you support).

I will not be slacking on Saturday morning though, along with Ross, Sandra and Bernice it will be business as usual at the gym who knows Sparrow Legs might make an appearance!!!

Big shout out to Scottish Widows for the £100 dona-tion much appreciated the charities will be very grateful.

Mick has been a busy guy this week check this lot out. Golf day; 4 April at Richlings Park. £75 includes breakfast lunch and dinner. Comedy night; May at Waterman's Arms, Eton £10 includes a comedian!!! Quiz Night; 8 June at Iver Village Hall, includes a fish supper only £10. Well done Mick you are putting the rest of us to shame. Mind you Ross has been in touch with David Lloyd Health Clubs who have said they will promote us on their Facebook page, which has 41,000 followers so that's got to be good news.

The saga of Mick and his cleats continues, first he manages to fall off in the kitchen whilst just trying them on. Then he braves the open road and comes a cropper within the first five miles, well it was a lot less than five miles but I won't elaborate on that one. Let us know if you had a fall first time in cleats. I know I did, I got to a roundabout stopped, went to put my foot down and didn't then ended up in a heap on the tarmac, everyone around was looking at me, slightly bewildered I made a swift exit like Del boy when he fell behind the bar in *Only Fools and Horses*.

We should be using our Twitter feed a bit more from now on so follow us please.

I can't give you the link as I'm pretty crap with the technical side of things, hopefully one of the clever team members will post it below.

The website will also be getting updated in the not too distant future, listing all event details and contacts for tickets, if it doesn't watch this space and I will try to do it on here.

Big thanks to all who have contacted us regarding the Ball, invitations will be coming out soon and displayed on here. It will be first come, first served I'm afraid, as we will sell this event out. Please let us know if you are interested and you will be notified first.

Finally thanks for reading comments always encouraged

Kevee

22/3/13

"Here's my story it's sad but true" that sounds like an old song lyric from the fifties, very apt at the moment, the country is pretty knackered, no one has any money, mind you the rest of Europe seems in a worse state. The weather is pretty sad too mid-March and it's snowing.

So what better way to cheer yourself up than have a night out at one of ROUTE 66 events? You get a two for one, experience a cheap night out and raising money for Help for Heroes and the Willow Foundation. Now that's what I call a bargain.

We had 910 views on the blog last week thanks to everyone who shared it; if your reading it please like our page, the more support the better, we want this to go viral so we can raise as much money as we can. Big shout out to Becky my daughter who shares everything we post on here and on twitter. The Herts Uni Rugby team have swelled the likes this week, well done guys and good luck Wednesday.

So what's the criac this week? Well H4H have a massive cycle ride planned 2 June, I believe get yourself on that one. Willows have a big cycle planned to on 21 July, we cycled it last year and it was a testing 60 miler.

31/3/13

Happy Easter to everyone, thanks for reading last week's blog over 2,000 views. Big thanks to Abi, Jess, Rod and Herts Uni Blogging Society for the shares it makes a big difference.

The Good Friday ride went well Ross and Danny putting 54 miles in. Mick had a few mechanical issues but has mastered the cleats!!!! Casey was due to ride but his aerodynamics were not very good due to his nose coming off worse with someone's elbow, whilst playing rugby for Herts Uni on Wednesday.

Mick has sorted another 100 square raffle, the top prize being a night in a London hotel with theatre tickets. £10 a ticket details to follow.

Ross has sorted the Ball poster; Danny has secured some top auction prizes; one being a trip to the top of Big Ben. Get your tickets ordered to avoid missing out.

Time is ticking away October seems to be sneaking up on us. Training is going well; most of the team have not been down the pub at all lately, the Chancellor of the Exchequer is wondering where he is going to make up the revenue shortfall!

We are still one rider short on the team so if you are up for a challenge please contact us, criteria as follows,

1. Can you pay for your trip?
2. Are you a team player?
3. Can you put up with me snoring?
4. Can you ride a bike?
5. Will you get extremely merry at the finish?

If you want to listen to Queen, Duran Duran, Robbie Williams or Adele on the Winnebago please do not apply.

If you are following the page [2,661 views last week] please tick the like box at the top of the page we really want to get this number up. We are giving away a free hoddie next weekend to one of our followers so like us to be in with a chance.

Cheers
Kevee

7/4/13
In the words of a great Rancid song *"Good morning heartache you're like an old friend come to see me again"* I think that sums up Saturday mornings at the

moment for Ross, me, Sandra and Bernice, circuits followed by spin with Kat, we love it but it hurts so good! (Or does it) The Sun has come out today so if the legs have anything left it will be a little ride out tomorrow.

What a week Breitling have been most generous in their support for the challenge and we are very grateful.

Mark and Ross have been meeting other prospective corporate partners.

Mick hosted a golf day in a snow blizzard, thanks to those who turned up.

We had a meeting with Carol from the Willow Foundation to discuss their up and coming cycling event (watch this space). We are all going to take part in that one.

New team photo coming soon. Help for Heroes are going to promote it on their website so great news.

The Ball tickets are starting to get reserved, so get in quick.

Thanks to Louise and Jacob for the donations, the amount raised is starting to go up now and that is what we really want.

As promised we are giving away a Hoddie and the winner is John Spashett, so please message us to claim your prize we hope you like yellow!!!

Gadget man Ross has got himself a helmet camera, as have I so he can capture the front of the bunch and I can do the scenery at the rear.

On a personnel note I'm knackered. I think I have been to the gym more in the last few months than in my entire life. I realise now if I had trained when I played rugby I may have made the second team at the Vees!!! Sandra is cycling with me to Paris in June and

I'm really looking forward to that, it should be good for the legs and will get me saddle fit for the seven-day challenge to come.

Thanks for reading and sharing

Kevee

13/4/13
'MARGARET THATCHER'

I thought that might catch your attention. It seems to me the whole nation is discussing Maggie. I don't want to get into that debate all I would say is she reminds me of a jar of Marmite; you either love it or hate it and there are not a lot of people in between.

It's a bit like fundraising your either good at it or you're not. As a group we are well off our original target at the moment. Perhaps our target was too high, perhaps the recession is having an effect or is it just everyone is taking part in fundraisers these days who knows.

As a group we are trying our hardest, organising events, sorting out merchandise, blogging and tweeting and hassling who ever we know. I must admit it has been a great journey so far and now we are into the last six months before we go, time seems to have ticked away quickly.

Everything is in place except the eighth elusive rider we can do it with seven but eight would be better, could it be you?

Over the last three month's I have discovered a fantastic new diet it's called exercise. It really is amazing; exercise then eat as much as you like of whatever you like and you still lose weight, bloody brilliant, can't believe I never thought of this before. Even one of my work client's commented, "You seem to have lost your belly Kevin," very nice of her to point that out to me I never realised it was that prominent!

That's it for this week visit our Facebook page for full listings of what we are up to in the next few weeks, follow us on Twitter, we have hit the 300 follower mark and are one off 400 on Facebook, so thanks to you all. If you have a spare moment please visit The Willow Foundation and Help for Heroes website's, our two chosen charities.

Cheers
Kevee

19/4/13
'Lyrca'
What's that all about? Middle age men in Lycra, hmm judging by our group photo last week the fashion police will be on our case very shortly. You pop along to your local bike shop and the assistant is very helpful 'Oh yes sir the sizes do come up a bit small try the XXL it's supposed to be a little tight,' yea right!

Then team member Mark is telling us to shave our legs, why? I can't imagine me and Ross turning up at the Verulamians rugby club third team dressing room with shaved legs and lycra shorts. You might get away with it in the first team, but the thirds you got to be joking.

Team photo shoot last week the magnificent seven became the furious five, well not really furious but fabulous five doesn't sound quite the same or five go cycling in Herts countryside that sounds more like an Enid Blyton novel.

After the photo's Casey, Ross, Dan and Mick embarked on a quick testosterone session Daniel had to bail early which left the other three to reminisce about last years Amsterdam and Brussels trip and the epic 112 miler. Unless you went wrong and it became the epic 118 miler, that was the day after Amsterdam bad planning.

Mick has been quoted as saying, 'The youngsters had me on the flat but on the hills I was king,' hence from now on Peroni Man becomes, 'King Of The Hills'.

A polka dot jersey will be heading his way.

Team rider news,

Andy and Mark have been a bit snowed under with things of late, so we're hoping to catch up with them soon.

Daniel is sorting out a clay pigeon shoot (great poster by his daughter).

Ross is looking to finalize the team line up by next week.

Casey has played his last game for Hertfordshire Uni Rugby team this week.

Mick is readying himself for a two-day cycle to Skipton (it's up north somewhere).

Big Dan, former rider but still very much a team member, is sorting some tech things out for us.

I just sit around and write a blog.

Thanks for the new likes 407 we're on a roll

Cheers
Kevee

26/4/2013

And then there we're eight Big Barry McGrath (Bazza) has joined the party and he seems like a nice geezer, we sealed the deal over a pint Monday night. I would like to say over a nice pint in a nice pub but alas it was not a nice pint and not a nice pub. It reminded me of the pub in *"An American Werewolf in London"* the locals gave us a few up and down looks it went very quiet, maybe they are not used to seeing people with yellow hair, or was it Rossy Boys suave sophisticated look? It might just have been we were not locals. I certainly won't be rushing back. Welcome on board Barry I promise we won't let Danny pick the venue for our next meet. I found myself listening to Kiss radio this week and those of you who know me well will be a little surprised to hear that. If you ever go spinning, for 45 minutes you get 72 BPM banging in your ear, which then goes to double beats and your legs are running at 144 revolutions, your brain doesn't quite think that quick and it all gets a bit confusing. *"Hill Climb"* and Rhianna is *shining bright like a bloody diamond* while me Ross and Casey are more reminiscent of a rather dull clapped out Ford Cortina with a dodgy starter motor, it wants to start you know it does but it just quite won't turn over. Kat's shouting, add another gear and I'm thinking I wish this bike were an automatic, I can't find another gear. At least my younger friends are impressed with my newfound knowledge of dance music.

The comedy night is sold out, fantastic news. Willows are still looking for riders for the big London bike ride get in contact with them, this event will be as big as The London Marathon in years to come, you could be taking part in the inaugural event and be raising money for a great cause.

Other News; I'm off to the Ian Swanston Charity Ball tomorrow night, always a good night and Anne really is the master at raising money I shall be trying to pick up a few tips.

Casey has been down the Welwyn Velodrome trying to steal a few yards on the rest of the team

Mick is abroad golfing, Ross is eying up a new bike (its to much money mate).

I need to speak to Mark and Andy, I have no idea what they are up to.

Danny is hanging out in weird pubs; Barry is probably boring everyone with talk about Route 66 like we have for a year and a half.

Cheers for reading and sharing

Kevee

2/5/13

"Where we at?"

This week – well tomorrow – we be at the sold out Comedy Night. That's all of us apart from Casey AKA Sparrow Legs who has his last exam then he will be off to do what students do best, go out and have a few sherbets. Only they don't these days they "pre drink" It seems everyone between the age of 18 – 25 pre drinks. I thought the idea was to go out for a drink but I'm informed I'm a bit of a dinosaur, it doesn't happen like that anymore. In fact I believe half of Hertfordshire has pre drunk at my house over the last four years. Pre drinking starts about eight and goes on till the taxis arrive about 11pm, if you're lucky. I like to have a few Peroni's and Samuel Adams Boston Lagers in stock, but

I always end up with a couple of cans of Fosters and three and a half cans of Tesco value lager which doesn't seem like a fair trade to me.

Mark has finished waxing his legs and will be in attendance Friday whilst Andy who has been working hard and putting some massive solo rides in will also be about (maybe that's why we call him the Camel because he's often out on his own or was it his rather peculiar look in his bib shorts in France? that's another story not for the faint hearted).

2 June sees some of the team taking part in the Hero Ride, this is a massive event for Help for Heroes, check it out on their website closing date for entries is Friday.

For the first time this year I missed training Saturday morning, as I had to work. I can't believe I was upset about this, have I turned into a fitness fanatic? Oh how things have changed. Ross is already trying to plan some future challenge but I think I will be all challenged out after October. Maybe the golf clubs will be a calling but I'm not really that old am I?

Hope you are all enjoying the blog feel free to comment below. Its 10 weeks in now and were getting between 1,100 and 2,100 views a week just on the blog with loads of hits on the page. If you haven't liked the page please do so and if you could share the blog with your friends we would appreciate that.

I'm hoping to get a few tips off the comedians tomorrow so I might be able to make next weeks a bit more amusing, who knows.

Cheers
Kevee

10/5/13

Star date 10/05/13. What's that all about? I'm off to see the new *Star Trek* movie to boldly go where no man has been before – Route 66 in a Winnebago cycling on/off for 7 days – we don't think anyone has done it this way before.

I can't make my mind up what to put in this week s blog I like to think it's amusing and witty, realizing after the comedy night my jokes are probably not that funny, although the comedians seemed to find my appearance highly amusing.

Lesson 1: do not sit to near to the front.

Lesson 2: try to blend in with the crowd! (Not sure that will ever happen).

Fund raising; we're nearly up to £10,000 thanks to all the students who have taken time out from pre-drinking to donate.

I'm very lucky because if you embark on a challenge and you have the support of your family you're halfway there. Thanks to Sandra, Bex and Bernice (adopted family), for always sharing the blog and putting up with Myself, K and Ross who have been talking about nothing else for the last year.

What's the team been up to this week?

Mick aka King of the hills is slipping into depression, his beloved Hornet's have not quite made it yet, hence he has been a bit quiet we will keep you posted on his state of mind.

Casey or Sparrow Legs as he is affectionately known is no longer a student he is looking for a bit of time out after suffering the affects of student life over the last three years. We like to call it detox.

Andy Gump is still going out cycling in Forrest fashion no plan he just keeps on going and going and going.

Mark declined the offer to resurrect his stand-up comic routine by doing a Houdini type illusion instead, he just vanished at 9.30pm.

Danny has been looking after the kids and trying to organize a ride out.

Big Bazza doesn't do Facebook much, so I can't keep tabs on him.

Rossy Boy is a bit under the weather he missed training this morning taking advantage of the fact Kat is on holiday he's probably thinking she won't find out, but she will because I will tell her.

Oh yes "Bombardier" beer and "Fuelled by Cakes" have been following us on Twitter they obviously know what sort of rider I am. Some of us like protein shakes (but to be honest if I want protein I'll have a steak) but beer and cakes, you can't argue with that.

Until next time

Kevee

19/5/13
This week it's all about the photo. The team finally managed to get together for our long awaited team photo. What a fine looking bunch of lads. Fitness levels are peaking as most of the team are starting to enjoy the glorious summer weather we have been having!!!!! In all fairness the team has not been out together as much as we would have liked, the weather being a factor as is work for everyone at the moment. The weather has improved so there will be less of an

excuse to take the easy option of the gym now. I say easy option only because our instructor Kat has been away and we have been slacking off a bit taking advantage of her absence.

The loveable Big Bazza is organising a trip to Newmarket races with Madness playing in the evening. To younger readers they were a Ska band back in the 80s not quite in the league of The Specials and they went a bit off track later in their career but they did know how to make a good video.

Danny has got another auction prise lined up; some sort of bush craft experience, what's that all about? I don't know but it seems a popular choice amongst some team members. If you want to get a fire started, use a lighter or a match that's why they were invented.

I have had a majorly busy week with work and last night Rossy Boy came over with his lovely wife to watch the Eurovision song contest, it could put you off music for life. What were we thinking 'Bonnie Tyler' let's hope she gets lost in France on the way home.

I'm sounding a bit moody this week but I'm not really I'm just completely knackered and I may have had a little too much wine last night, so I'm off out with Sandra for a bit of fresh air.

Laters
Kevee

24/5/13
I have decided not to do my usual blog this week in light of Drummer Lee Rigby's brutal murder on the streets of our capital city. My thoughts are with his family and

friends, I cannot begin to comprehend what they must be going through.

Friends who know me well will realise that I am not normally lost for words but I was horrified by the events unfolding on the television this week and it has left me numb and speechless.

The Team is even more determined than ever to raise as much money as we can for our chosen charities and we will be proudly wearing our Help for Heroes wristbands and shirts whenever we hit the road and all the way to LA.

Thanks to everyone who has donated in the last couple of weeks James, Becky, Paul, Jo, Pam, Del, The Pages and David at Marshall D.G. Your support is appreciated.

I will leave you with this thought 'TWO WRONGS DO NOT MAKE A RIGHT'

Stay calm everyone justice will prevail

Kevee

1/6/13
Rod's Blog
Thanks for all the highly amusing comments regarding my current hairstyle this week, rest assured the said "Rod Stewart" lookalike style will be leaving my head in the not too distant future.

I have been charged this week with getting some useful information in to the blog, this may prove a bit tricky because I'm about as useful as a handbrake on a canoe when it comes to tech stuff, so links may or may not work.

I used to laugh at my Dad when he couldn't use the remote on the video recorder back in the day, now I find myself not able to do things which 10-year-old kids don't seem to have any trouble with. At least I can load my own blog up that's a start.

The big news this week is Shorter Rochford Cycles have sponsored us to the tune of 24 cycle shirts, which is incredible news and we are truly grateful for that.

Up and coming events posters will be loaded up to the page, so please visit if you haven't already.

Only 12 tables left for the ball so please contact us if you wish to attend.

The holiday season is about to start for the team Ross is off to Ibiza to reunite with his youth he has been down the gym this week in preparation for all the energy he will be using up Gangnam style dancing!!!!

Myself and Sandra are cycling to Paris in a couple of weeks, which is where I met Mick and Andy two years ago. I'm hoping I will meet some more characters this time as I made some life-long friends the last time.

To all my friends I keep blowing out the last few weeks, I apologise for that, I have been off the beer of late, things may change this week with the The British and Irish Lions tour about to start. Who knows it might inspire me to pull the old Verulamians shirt back on next season (after October obviously). I'm not missing the pain I feel all week after a game though, so I'll maybe stick to cycling, although my backside would argue that the saddle is more pain than any hit you get in Rugby.

By the way please sponsor us at the link below Help for Heroes and the Willow foundation need your support Thanks to Chris Greenwood for his generous donation.

Cheers
Kevee

8/6/13

'Demented Are Go' anyone?

I have been trying to work out a playlist for the trip, not necessarily for everyone else to listen to but so I can switch myself off from everyone now and again. Eight tired riders and two tired drivers could get a bit tense if someone decides to play a bit of Abba or Duran Duran at four in the morning. We're heading through the middle of America, so I thought a bit of Rockabilly or Pyscobilly. So maybe a bit of *"Demented are Go"* *"The Guana Batz"* and *"The Milkshakes"* if you do not know these bands I won't be that surprised. Heading in to LA a bit of Surf music not the *"The Beach Boys"* but the now Legendary *"Palominos"* Hertfordshire's premier surf band from 1985!!!! Or shall we stick to a bit of Calvin Harris loved by spinning classes all over. Rossey boy will be after a bit of house music after his trip to Ibiza last week. Any suggestions welcome below we need a theme tune to keep us going best suggestion will receive a free route 66 T-shirt.

Mick and Mark have been out of action carrying a couple of injuries this week best to have them now rather than on the trip.

Danny boy is doing the Blenheim triathlon today, good luck to him.

Andy has been talking to a well-known phone manufacturer about communications for the trip. Big Baz is practicing his skanking routine for the Madness gig. Casey is working seven days a week to pay for his trip!!! and I have been sitting on my arse writing a blog!!!

Sandra has been away this week looking after her mother, who we hope gets better soon so I have taken on the motherly roll of hoovering, cooking, tea, etc. Needless to say the local takeaway did very well as did the vacuum cleaner, which I thought deserved a nice little holiday. Unfortunately we broke the washing machine but Sandra managed to fix that upon her return. Dishwashers are not as good as I thought either, apparently they don't load and unload themselves, someone needs to look into that oversight. Well she's back now and I'm sure she missed us! Only joking I have cooked some wonderful meals this week thank god the sun came out, I don't mind standing beside the BBQ watching things cook having a cheeky beer; it's what Dads do isn't it?

That is about it this week we are all training hard individually team rides are starting next month. If you want to tag along with us keep checking back here our website is struggling to get information updated so we will post on here.

Thanks to Steve from Travis Perkins for the donation and thanks to everyone reading the Facebook and Twitter feeds, nearly 3,000 hits a week cheers everyone

Kevee

18/6/13
Lycra Fetish
After a meeting in the local last week Big Bazzas lycra obsession came to light.

We were discussing the new cycling shirts being supplied to us by Shorter Rochford Cycles (what a nice bunch of guys, go check them out) when Bazza chipped in telling us about his new Rapha cycling shirt. I can safely say we are now all experts on the said tops, did you know that they have a luxurious feel, the fit just kind of tucks in all around you, it helps you cut through the air at a greater speed!!! This is the best bit, "It's like pulling on your first Fred Perry, you walk down the road with your chest all puffed out its wonderful." In conclusion I think I'm buying the wrong gear I pull on my top, look in the mirror and think I wish I hadn't had so many beers the last three months. I have to confess I have purchased a Rapha Team Sky T-shirt and I can't knock it. My father-in-law always used to say buy cheap buy twice and I think he is right. Big Bazza is certainly getting a lot of use out of his we think he even wears it to bed, but that is another story.

Other news we had a long wet day Saturday at Brookmans Park, but a good time was had by all thanks to everyone who supported us.

I'm off on a London to Paris ride this week with Sandra and I'm looking forward to getting a few miles in the old legs. Sandra is really excited about it!!!

Not sure what the other guys are up to this week, four of them are carrying some sort of injury, best to get that out of the way now rather than October.

If you want to sponsor Sandra on her cycle to Paris please do so on the Route 66 teams Virgin site as she would like to help The Willow Foundation and Help for Heroes thanks again to Jo who already has.

I'll keep you posted on how the trips going I know I will be eating well as you do on all Skyline trips and if I can meet some people like the ones I met cycling to Paris and Amsterdam on previous trips, I know I'm in for a good time and the odd cheeky beer.

Kevee

22/6/13

BONJOUR

Well this week has not been a Route 66 week for me I have been cycling to Paris with Sandra. I'm not too sure what the guys have been up to as I have just returned home. David Lloyd did a great piece for us on Facebook this week so we're getting the message about the trip out there. David Lloyd also did a great job on Sandra getting her fitness up for the Paris trip.

London to Paris on a bike what's it like? If you ever want to try it, try it with Skyline Events because you don't have to think about anything, they sort it all out for you. You basically turn up and ride your bike, they ship your bag, water and feed you, plan your route for you and even let you have a few beers on route.

I'm glad to know they are sorting all our logistics out for Route 66, so all we have to do is ride. Mind you they do tell the odd white lie about the terrain you may encounter, calling massive hills slight undulations but that is all part of the careful planning as to not dampen your spirits.

I must be tired tonight as I'm reading this blog back and it is not that funny maybe it never is that funny who knows!!!

I have learnt one thing this week, my fitness is not quite where I want it to be, so the bike will be getting a bit more time on the road over the coming weeks.

I have cycled this week with people aged 18 to 70 some trained some didn't but all 73 of them were a pleasure to ride with, no whinging, just getting on with the job in hand. Sometimes you realise that the world isn't such a selfish self-obsessed place and people do generally care about others.

28/6/13

It's Friday, its five o clock, it's crackerjack, or is it just another Kevee mundane Friday blog?

You all know the format by now, I write a blog about 2,000 people read it and if we are lucky we get one comment and a few likes. We also always get one negative feedback whether it's the same person every week who knows.

I usually plug the people who have helped us out, Shorter Rochford Cycles, Breitling Watches, Skyline events. I then crack on and tell you about up and coming events we have planned. Training – who's been up to what? Who hasn't been up to much? Who's injured who isn't?

Try and crack a joke about student's and the drinking habits they have, that always seems to get a few likes.

Make fun of one of the team (in a very nice manner of course). Always get the reason for why we are doing it in, to raise funds for Help For Heroes and The Willow Foundation. Talk a little about myself and usually about the work I have done at the gym or how I have become a crap drinker these days, not able to drink more than about three pints in one go.

But this week I'm not going to mention any of the above I'm just sitting here thinking 14 weeks to go until seven days in a Winnebago. 24/7 riding, sleeping, riding, eating and after about three days probably getting a bit cranky. I'm starting to panic a bit will I be able to keep up with the other riders will I let them down. What if it takes eight days rather than seven?

You know what though I am so looking forward to this trip out in the middle of nowhere with your mates not a care in the world it can't get much better than that.

Well it could you could be cycling for Team Sky in the Tour de France tomorrow, or pulling on a Lions shirt to beat the Aussies, or driving in the British Grand Prix, or the best of all spending time with your loved ones but apart from that, it doesn't get any better than this does it?

Have a good weekend everyone

Kevee

7/7/13

Hanging out the back

Yep that was me last Sunday I went out with the bigger boys Rossy, Dan and Bazza. "Oh yes Kevee we know you're a bit tired after Paris last week were just taking a gentle ride around Hertfordshire." Yea right 56 miles up and down, flat out, well I was flat out, Bazza wasn't even sweating. I managed to keep up sort of for the first 35–40 then seemed to blow a gasket. Jesus it's enough to put you off cigars!!! Seriously though them boys can motor, I need to up my game a bit.

The sun has been out for a couple of days so I'm calling it summer at last. Everyone I know has been so fed up that they have all booked holidays abroad to get a bit of sun, the ironic thing is it's going to be sunny here now for a few weeks, so most of us will miss our summer, you've got to laugh really.

I think the sun has a massive effect on people, the mood of the nation seems to lift overnight the old BBQ gets fired up, the Pimms comes out and it seems everyone and his dog is out cycling these days. It really is amazing how Brad winning the Tour and Olympic time trial has turned us into cycling fanatics.

Casey had his 21st birthday this week so I've been a bit preoccupied. A mass of friends converging at our house yesterday for a pre going out BBQ I think they had all gone by about 11pm and I'm sure the neighbours appreciated that fact. Beer Pong, what's that all about? It seems to be very loud and involves a lot of drinking; the parents among you may have come across the said game if you have ever let your kids have a party at home.

We're all off to see Skyline this week to finalize logistics then it's all systems go.

Some of the guys are already starting to think about what we can do next year I'm thinking a nice relaxing holiday with Sandra maybe a cycle across Vietnam I won't tell her just yet though!!!!

Cheers
Kevee

12/7/13
"A cracking week was had by all." It's been busy, busy, busy, the last few days. "Oh Danny Boy" had great success at the shoot he organised, pulling in £585 for the charities great work fella.

Big Bazza is cycling coast to coast as I write this and has the Race Day organised for next Friday. Ross and Bernice have the Tea Party this Sunday, details are all on this page. Mark is sorting out a tyre sponsorship deal The Camel has been burying himself in training because he has lost a shed load of weight. The boy wonder Casey, he is working flat out to pay for his trip. Mick is doing loads of work in the background and making sure he keeps us all focused on fundraising. Skyline have been to the States and driven the route we will be taking. On that note they did mention we might come across the odd Rattlesnake, I thought John Wayne had shot all the Snakes back in the fifties!!!! Thanks to Sally from Skyline for picking a great team leader in Greg for the trip he seemed to fit in really well and after the meeting he accompanied us to the local, always a good sign. I have been told to mention the Ball, tickets really are moving fast, if you have indicated you want some you need to get in touch with one of the team to confirm you are still coming. We need to start collecting all outstanding money so a quick response would be most welcome.

Its an early blog this week, sometimes its early, sometimes its late, but I'm feeling a bit unwell today hence the blog is early. Before all my female friends start thinking I have a bout of man flu I will inform you its more of I don't want to be to far from the smallest room in the house type of illness. I nice quiet night in tonight I think.

Any would be companies still wanting to get involved please contact Ross as I believe he is about to push the button on the shirts we will be wearing. I think we have about 10 companies now so the shirt is looking cool. I would like to publicly thank my mate Ross today. I know I moan at him when he makes me go to the gym or go out on the bikes to train. I sometimes wonder if he's trying to kill me off, with all these challenges he insists I do. I dread to think what he will come up with next. But I'm lucky to be still fit enough to do things, some of my friends are starting to suffer with all sorts of complaints perhaps it's my age group. So maybe I should keep going as long as I can. I promised one of my friends years ago

I would give in and go on a cruise when I'm fifty, but you know what there's life in the old dog yet, so I won't be setting foot on that cruise ship for a few more years. Please spare a second to share this blog, the more people who go to our page the more chance we have of raising more money for The Willow Foundation and Help for Heroes.

Cheers
Kevee

28/9/13
Sorry for the delay, last week was the first time I missed a blog since I started writing them. I sneaked away with Sandra for a few days for a bit of relaxation, we did hire a couple of bikes and spent quite a lot of time on them but I felt quite relaxed.

Lots of things to update you on so I will dive straight in, The Willow Foundation have given us a place on the big Ride London 100 taking place next Sunday, Mick has recovered from injury and will be taking part and with Box Hill included in the ride, its only fair our very on King of the Mountains is unleashed.

Help for Heroes have put our event on their website check it out it's always worth a visit.

Donations are starting to gain momentum thank you all for your support.

Continental have very kindly supplied us with 24 gatorskin tyres, according to our logistics team were going to need good tyres some of the terrain is a bit rough.

If anyone reading this who cycles a lot at night could suggest good lights I would appreciate that, we certainly want to be seen as we're riding along. You might think it a bit odd that we haven't done much night riding considering we will be riding 24/7 but it makes it more of a challenge doesn't it?

I managed to get out with a few of my mates Friday night who seem to think I have gone cycling mad. I tried to assure them that once this challenge is complete I probably won't want to go anywhere near a bike for a very long time, ha ha that won't happen.

The question everyone keeps asking is what has been the hardest part of this challenge? I've been pondering on this all morning the obvious answer is the ride itself, lets face it if you are a good cyclist who rides everyday to work then goes out both days at the weekend, eats the right food and doesn't drink much you may think it is not much of a challenge at all. We don't do that, finding time to train whilst working and not having the energy to go out when you know you need to, that is more of where we are at. Organizing events and trying to get people to attend now that is a challenge. You can only ask so much of your friends. Updating the website Twitter and Facebook, trying to write an interesting blog! Saving up to pay for the trip and kit for the bikes. It makes you realize that people who work for charities have a very rewarding job, but the pressure on them must be immense with so many charities about all trying to survive in the current financial climate, its small wonder that many don't survive. One of the tasks the team gave me was to be our Willow contact as I live not far from them it has been a great experience for me. Carol our contact works extremely hard, if she's not in the office, she's at an event or tweeting a Friday shout-out to all their supporters. I don't know how she keeps track of who's doing what and when.

That is enough from me this week hope to see some of you out supporting Mick next Sunday.

Kevee

4/8/13
Another week another Blog
PRUDENTIAL RIDE LONDON 100
Well done Micky Boy (aka Peroni Man aka King of the Boxhill) If you don't get to ride yourself what better way to enjoy yourself on a Sunday afternoon than to pop into London and watch your mates and thousands of others raise loads of money for their chosen charities cycling down The Mall. Boris I think this cycling extravaganza will be around for many years to come.

I just had a text from Mick and he's enjoying a well-earned recovery bottle of Peroni. Well done to former L2P friends who also took part today Rob, Rob and Neil.

Danny Boy, Rosco Sparrow Legs and myself popped out for a 50 miler yesterday and the less said about that the better because I think I left my legs at home in bed, the other lads were cutting me a lot of slack. I might be banished to the lonely night shift on Route 66 if I don't improve!!!!

Please help me out a bit here; Bernice is giving me and all the rest of the team an awful lot of grief about the ball. If you have indicated you are coming can you please contact one of us to clarify payment details, we need to confirm numbers and pay for the event next week.

We leave Chicago on 4 October and if you're getting tired reading all the blogs I am going to be writing why not give yourself a break and take part in The Willow Foundation 10k on 6 October, it is a fantastic event held annually in the grounds of Hatfield House. All details are on their Website. It's a real family day out much better than dragging the kids around Sainsbury's.

Thanks for reading, I'm hoping Mick will put up a piece about the joy and pain of today's ride so I'm keeping the blog short.

I will leave you with this thought; we build new roads, they get filled up, we add extra lanes they get filled up, why not stop building more roads and build more cycle routes? You never know if the routes actually joined up with other routes they might get filled up as well, simples right!!!

Cheers
Kevee

9/8/13
Hope you enjoyed Mick's account of his ride last week. I am trying to get all the guys to write a blog before we go to give an insight as to what we are all like. You should all know what I am like by now. I have been boring you all with the same jokes for the last few months. After reading Mick's account it would appear that my creative, descriptive, writing may not be, after all. It's more like a couple of sentences, loosely punctuated, scribbled together in a tea break. A sort of; here you are take it or leave it approach.

Hmm the lads always want me to ask for your support, well by reading this you're giving your support. 500 followers I think is pretty amazing. Big up the challenge Kevee, big up what?

I have to get on a bike and ride it for seven days maybe eight or nine if things go pear shaped. The thing with raising money is it's hard work; you either can do it well or not. Mick and Andy have proved they can do it and their friends have been very supportive over the last two years attending quiz after quiz, Zumba after Zumba I know my mates are not really into that sort of thing especially down the rugby club, the only question that needs to be asked is how many pints can one consume per hour after the game? As for the Zumba we have all done a bit of limbo dancing toward the end of a club supper, does that count?

What have I learned over the last two years?

1   I enjoy writing a blog as much as I enjoy cycling (that is a worry).
2   My arse is not designed for saddles!
3   I am not as competitive as the rest of the team (we finish when we finish as long as it's together).
4   My use of a computer has improved up to the level of a nine-year-old!!!
5   I am very fortunate to have such a supportive family and friends.

In conclusion eight weeks today we start in Chicago, Nine weeks today it should be over, will I be relieved or maybe slightly saddened it's the end? Only time will tell. It will be a nice story to converse to the grandchildren if I have any, "The week I cycled Route 66" it's got a romantic musical past that sits nicely with me.

In the words of an old Palominos song I'll be *"Talking Bout You Babe"* for the rest of my days

Cheers
Kevee

PS Next week old Sparrow legs himself (Casey) is due to write a blog I have a feeling it may be a tad shorter than Mick's something like, "Hi I'm Casey, I'm cycling, yes on a bike, yes in America, can mum come and iron my clothes and do my washing? Will I be able to eat all day? Will I be able to keep up with my dad?

Stay tuned for these and many more questions like them to be answered over to you KC,

18/8/13
"Work." What's that all about?
Seems to get in the way of a lot of things, you can't train because you're at work. You can't train because you're too tired from work and if you don't work you can't train because you can't afford a decent bike.

Life is all about getting the balance right. Someone said to me this week, "Why go on holiday, what have you got left at the end of it only a memory and you might forget that, it is far better to have the money in the bank." I think it is great we all have different views on life but I have to admit the things in life I have never forgotten are the holiday's I have been on right back to when my Mother and Father used to take me to Butlin's when I was just a wee nipper. My point being, with this is we have spent nigh on two years planning and talking about this challenge it is something I will never forget. Financially I would be better off not taking part, but honestly who wouldn't want to be part of this challenge to ride the iconic Route 66? I'll take the memory any day.

Kevee

25/8/13

Pants

This seems to be a very topical subject at the moment Rossco's blog this week and Casey's blog of last week have featured the subject of my pants and the where-abouts of them. I never realized that my underpants were the concern of so many people. What is it going to be like on the Winnebago? Will I have to sneak to the toilet to change my underwear to avoid any more unwanted chit-chat plastered all over Facebook? Maybe it's a jealousy thing, are my pants just more trendy than everyone else?

It's great the lads are updating everything in their blogs it enables me to write what I want. I'm down in Cornwall for the weekend, thought I might get a couple of rides in but I've only managed to get a couple of Cornish pints in at the moment, but I shall make a big effort tomorrow. I can see why Julie and Joe were good on the hills in L2P they were either training a lot or just drinking an awful lot of cider to numb the pain. (Probably the latter.)

Everyone is fit at the moment or should I say injury free, fit might mean different things to different people some people call walking to the pub keeping fit while others only count climbing Kilimanjaro as measuring your fitness levels, it's a good job we're all different it would be a boring life if we were all the same.

I was asked this week what would I consider was my greatest achievement in life I found this a very difficult question to answer take a minute to think to yourself what is your greatest achievement it's hard isn't it?

Being a good Father, that has to be an achievement, although kids usually take after their Mum. Running the London Marathon after giving up smoking, that felt like an achievement.

Cycling to Paris, my arse thought that was an achievement I could do without.

Being in a band and getting people to come and watch us, that ranks highly.

Helping to coach youth Rugby and football teams that was hard work. Would that class as an achievement? Probably not.

Being a captain of a third team down the rugby club and getting people to turn up and play now that is an achievement.

I don't think there is one defining moment in my life that could make me say yes that is my greatest achievement. To be a great sports star or run a multi-million pound business, or be a successful politician you have to be 100% focused and friends and family might get overlooked a little along your path to greatness. So I suspect my greatest achievement in life will always be just being me, not outstanding at anything really, but I'll have a go and enjoy a drink with a few mates and family after it and tell everyone if only I had focused a bit more I could have been a legend!

Cheers
Kevee

30/8/13

Be-Jesus five weeks today

Unlike Andy I'm looking in the mirror thinking another few pounds being shed wouldn't go a miss.

Rossco is cooking my tea tonight I'm expecting a nice healthy meal washed down with maybe a glass of red. He's a bit of a gourmet chef is our Ross, as is Mick, I'm more of your traditional male chef, bacon and egg or anything that includes potatoes especially chips. I'm so looking forward to the meals en route I certainly won't go hungry and the American's love a big portion don't they? A large coke here is like a mini coke over there, have you seen the size of them cups? It's like two pints of beer.

Some of the team are struggling with injuries at the moment, let's hope everyone is fit for the start or we might have to get Bernice and Sandra into some lycra, hmm that's another story not for this blog.

I have been told I'm getting too philosophical of late in my blogs, pondering on life and my humour seems to be degenerating, what's that all about? I thought I was hilarious I only have to turn up somewhere and everyone is laughing about my clothes or current hairstyle. I saw my old friends Jo and Keith this week and they reminded me of Keith's 50th and the dance off between myself, Keith, Casey and Greg, them young boys have a lot to learn, me and Keith romped it, there's life in the old dogs yet! We could have taken the easy option and admitted old age was sneaking up, but no chance. We still have the moves and choose to use them. When the boys were playing rugby and we were on one of Tony Maile's tours in France, I remember having to all get on the coach at twelve to take the boys back to the accommodation.

Myself, Keith and O'Grady waved the coach off and headed to a blues bar and had a whale of a time little did we know Greg and Casey headed back into town that night (now that's just disrespectful) but hey if we can't find a blues bar in Chicago it's time to get the pipe and slippers out.

I don't seem to have much of a theme this week maybe I will focus a bit more next week, your guess is as good as mine.

Cheers
Kevee

5/9/13
The Last Supper, well not quite but it tees me up for another Kevee Blog.

The whole team got together last night for a final briefing. We had many things to discuss starting with the kit list. Bloody hell; I was thinking I could just turn up and ride my bike, wrong. No detail was left to chance right down to super glue and chamois cream, I'm hoping no one will get those two muddled up that could cause an unenforced stop at a local hospital. You do need to be organised and Andy really was on the ball, good work fella. He is a shadow of his former self. I think the shares in Guinness must be plummeting, he's been training hard on his own and you can see the difference.

The Ball details were finalised, some wanted this, some wanted that, but I'm sure you will all be impressed with the outcome. You will be glad to hear only Mick and Ross will talk, as the general consensus was all eight of us rambling on might take up the entire night. You've all heard a great deal from me over the last six-month's so I will be taking a back seat and enjoying the proceedings.

Mark is fully recovered from his op and back in training which is a big plus.

Danny Casey and Barry are our jokers in the pack and you can afford to be, if you cycle like them. I'm sure the dry sense of humour will be a big advantage on the desert night shifts. I just wish Bazza would stop going on about Rattle Snakes

Its Danny Boys Blog this week make sure you read it, his wife has worked hard on it or so he tells us.

Oh I nearly forgot The Last Supper that will be in LA hopefully with the whole team finishing uninjured, still taking to each other and having raised a load of money for Help for Heroes and The Willow Foundation five weeks tomorrow we shall know!!

Cheers
Kevee

11/9/13
Disastrous or a fun day out?
Last week seven of the team cycled to Brighton, we had punctures, Flu and it was raining cats and dogs.

First up myself, Bazza, Oh Danny Boy, Sparrow legs and Rossco met up at 4.30am (no that's not a typo 4.30am at South Mimms service station), to cycle to Clapham Common to meet up with The Camel and Peroni Man, only thing no Rossco. The poor old fella had a puncture on route in the pitch black, when he finally arrived the air turned blue with his torrent of expletives explaining his late arrival.

Off we set and I must say it was a very pleasant ride into town, all working together as a team enjoying the quiet roads apart from the bloke who decided to turn straight into us at the traffic lights not realising he was on the wrong side of the road, maybe he was on his way back from a nightclub.

We met the others and decided not to eat in favour of registering at the start and hitting the road, this would prove to be a big error.

We set off together but the pace was too fast for me as my man flu was giving me a torrid ride, but Casey and Andy slowed up and dragged me round to lunch. If you know Casey you know he has to eat virtually 24/7 and by the time we reached lunch you would have thought he had not eaten for a month. The whole team ate together then set off in different groups as some of the team were rushing as they planned to cycle back and get 150 miles under their belts.

I cycled on with Sparrow and Rossco and was feeling much better after lunch but Rossco had not taken on much food and suffered bad from cramps pretty much for the remainder of the ride.

Sandra and Bex were bringing the van down to pick us up but yes you guessed it they had a puncture and the tyre got shredded but as with most new vehicles' these days you don't get a spare you get a repair kit, a lot of good that is if your tyre is shredded, hence they were going to be late to meet us.

Bazz Mick and Andy didn't stay in Brighton long as they wanted to cycle back, but along came the rain, bad visibility and failing light batteries and after getting to

Gatwick they threw in the towel and hopped on the train. Dan had gone to meet his family and friends so he fared well. We met up with the girls and had a well-earned Sunday lunch in the pub and very nice it was to. We should have stayed longer as I think it took longer to drive back than it took us to ride down.

In conclusion what have we learned, well the Do it for Charity London to Brighton Cycle is a well organised fun trip.

You can cycle with man flu albeit a bit slowly.

We need better clothes for rain and back up batteries for lights.

We defiantly need to fuel up more on the trip and never ride on an empty stomach, although we should know the latter but at 4am in the morning food is not that appealing.

Lastly the team worked well together not letting anyone get isolated which bodes well for the desert stint.

Oh and we still haven't cycled with Mark, but he assures us he can really move and he's doing the guest blog this week so keep your eye out for that Friday.

Kevee

19/9/13
Argh the Ball is upon us.

What a fantastic Ball we have organised, it is so easy to sort these things out first you find a venue (thanks Sandra for that), then you sort a top band (thanks Bernice for that), get a good deal on the venue and pick the food (well done Sandra and Bernice), badger the riders for names of their guests (we'll give Bernice that one, oh and don't forget the table plans), sort decorations, timings etc (well them things are best left to the girls). Like I was saying nothing to it, organising a ball; me and the boys have found it quite stress free in fact we are all looking forward to a nice relaxed evening.

On a serious note we are hoping this will be our best fundraiser so far. Looking at ticket sales it already is.

Thanks Bernice and Sandra, without you two I don't think we would have got this off the ground, in fact I know we wouldn't have.

On a less serious note all eight riders are determined to ensure all our friends and family who are parting with hard-earned cash to come to this event will be thoroughly entertained. All riders will participate in drinking champagne, larger and wine, this will be followed by encouraging family and friends to join them on the dance floor, I must admit I haven't seen the other guys dance myself so I'm looking forward to that.

We have an MP attending, so we all have to behave ourselves.

We have the voice of TV cycling coming along, who might be 'pedalling squares' himself on his way home.

Big Bazza is going to nurse his hangover on Sunday by giving us a blog I'm not giving him any stick this week as I have noticed the other riders have been giving me a fair bit the last few weeks in their blogs and Barry is known to have a bit of a sharp wit so he's getting no ammunition from me.

Then that's it, you've heard from all eight of us, the time for talking is nearly over, the time for cycling is nearly upon us. Let the adventure begin.

Kevee

26/9/13

On a serious note, "The Last Kevee Blog."

Well here we go we're off on Wednesday so this is the last blog before we leave.

When we hit the mother road on the fourth, who knows how I will be feeling, the other guys will almost certainly want to be updating things as well so you may be getting an overload of team Route 66 blogs.

The idea of the blog was to get our challenge talked about by as many people as possible, also to keep updates of events and team training progress.

I have tried to keep them short, factual and dare I say a little tongue in cheek and I would like to think I have given it a good go, over thirty thousand hits which is truly amazing.

I would like to thank everyone who has helped us along the way especially all the riders who for various reasons have had to pull out.

How am I feeling this week? A little strange actually. Casey is taking part with me, which is great Sandra is coming over to support us, but my daughter, Bex being the cleverest out of us graduated last year and got herself a job as a teacher and due to the timings is unable to be with us. My daughter is a truly amazing person she has had to listen to us talking about this trip for nearly two years, has she been jealous? No. Has she sulked? No. Would she like to be coming? Of course she would. So what has she done? Ah ha, I will tell you every single blog I have put up here she shares with her friends, any comments she likes, any event she brings all her mates. Take the Ball; straight away she informs us she will fill a table (and does). Then she signs up for The Willow 10k insisting it will keep the interest going. So thanks Bex my unsung hero.

In conclusion,

Thanks to everyone who has sponsored us, came to the ball, have given us free kit or just liked our page and a massive thanks to all my friends who have personally supported me, I will try my best not to let anyone down.

See you in LA

Kevee

22/10/13

Well I made it home and even made it to work today, but was totally useless as my mind was willing but my body felt like it was still on Route 66 somewhere.

I'm going to keep it brief as the real story is about 200 pages long and I'm saving that for another day.

It was hard, we can all do multi day cycle's of 100 plus miles a day, stopping for coffee and lunch but nothing we could have done in training could have prepared us for this. If anyone out there is thinking of doing this challenge, start in LA and cycle east with the wind behind you it might save you a day or two. We had times where we had to draft the RV to keep moving, pedalling downhill is not much fun.

The crew of six who had led trips up Kilimanjaro, cycled Vietnam, walked the great wall in China etc., said this was the hardest trip they have ever been involved with. The guys were constantly navigating driving cooking and moaning about the smell of us lot from day one. (Hygiene levels with 14 blokes on two camper vans may have slipped a little during the seven days.)

We started early to avoid traffic but still managed to nearly have a crash 20 yards from the start with an irate American refusing to move his car an inch in reverse for half an hour. We cycled the first 20 miles together then stopped to get into pairs to continue, one of the team taking a leak up against a wall in a car park, only to be surprised by the sheriff deciding that was not the right thing to do with a RV with a toilet sitting beside him (first lesson learned only take a leak in an appropriate location).

The first day was a scorcher but the nights were cold, myself and Casey managing to get lost at night ended up with me taking a tumble. Danny Boy had got the flu bad but unbelievably kept on getting up to do his stint, how he continued I will never know.

Sleeping arrangements were all over the place you often found yourself in a pre-warmed bed with dribble all over the shared pillows. Big Bazza and Casey often snuggling up together in the double bed at the back due to the fact the bunk beds were about 4 foot 2 inches long. Andy liked the double room too and was the only cyclist to unpack properly and claim all the wardrobe space. The night he tried to get Casey out of bed to make it had me in stitches listening in the bunk.

Andy, "Come on Casey let's make the bed."

Casey, "No it's alright."

Andy, "Come on Case we need to sort it out."

Casey, "Well I'm happy with it."

Andy. "No we need to sort it out."

This went on till I fell asleep I still don't know the outcome.

We were doing ok with hardly any punctures or mechanicals which was a miracle considering some of the dirt tracks we were riding on. I think Kenny was worrying that Steve and Ian needed more to do, so he reversed the RV into a Sign post, the only thing being the bikes were on the bike rack at the back of the RV resulting in Marks pride and joy coming off somewhat worse than the sign post. Poor old Mark, having had the close encounter with the police, being attacked by dogs, he now found himself bike less. Ross had got very cold on the nightshift and was struggling to get warm; his legs were like blocks of ice for about two hours after his stint he should have jumped in the double bed with the others and stole a bit of warmth.

Day four was a great stint for me and Casey, rolling hills beautiful day with no wind unlike the night shift to follow with extreme wind in your face. Casey jumped in with Baz and Dan to do a ten-mile time trial at the end of our day stint. The forward van was further than anticipated. Bazza is like a machine, he just churns the big gear, he really was the top cyclist for me and his constant jokes kept me going day in and day out and Dan that flu wouldn't shift but a Bacon never gives in.

I suppose it was inevitable but the Tuesday turned out to be our toughest day as a team. Sleep deprivation and slipping behind on our goal of seven days caused a few minor disagreements. There is a section of the old route, which splits into two. One climbs up to Santa Fe a full on climb for mile after mile whilst the other takes a short cut on the flat; both routes are classed as historic Route 66 so either way would still be legitimate. Being in two vans and someone always on the road a decision was made to bypass Santa Fe and make up some time. The trouble was some of us wanted to do the climb and stick to the original plan so that's what we did. In hindsight we should have taken time out as a team to discuss this but it didn't happen but hey we're glad we did it now.

Andy and Mick had pretty much all of their stint climbing, it was a constant, gruelling climb. I've had the pleasure of cycling with those two before and they just keep going and going the level of determination is second to none. I think they always wonder why they do these things and raising money is what they do and this must give them the determination to get through. Casey and myself had the next stint and we had the rollers up and down but the wind cutting us to bits. Casey had pulled me round for four days but today he finally realised I could take a turn on the front maybe not as fast as him but he would get a breather. I had thanked him for helping me out and he turned and said you've been helping me out for 21 years Dad, it was a special moment for me. That night was a scary ride, I'll save that bit.

The Interstate, this can be like the M25 on a Monday morning and you guessed right some of Route 66 is now an Interstate. Some sections you are not allowed to cycle on and we had to skip two short sections not able to find an alternative.

As we waited for Andy and Mick to swap over it seemed to take ages then I realised that I was nearly getting blown over by a crosswind. We took over and it was horrendous luckily the wind was blowing us away from traffic. The roadwork section proved a little testing to say the least. Ross and Mark were on after us, still on the interstate, but the wind was proving a hazard and they decided to abandon a small section, as it was too dangerous to continue.

Reports of snow coming into Flagstaff that night kept us on our toes. Luckily we were ahead of it. Casey and me set off and it was the worst weather we encountered. The wind was sideways and it was lashing it down. Steve pulled up beside us and told us to get in the van Casey was having none of it and we rode side by side singing songs and laughing. When I got off I couldn't move my toes or fingers. We sort of showered (a slight dribble that loosely resembled a shower) once thawed out we sat and ate jam on toast for an hour.

The last day and Bazza, Dan and Casey with Will and Greg all climbed the mountain pass a great morning with both buses coming together for an hour. The crew were as much part of the team as we were and everyone looked forward to their sleep in the front bus with James' careful driving!!! (Sorry James although he did sit behind you like glue if he was in the back bus).

Next we rode straight roads forever, the Romans must have built these roads.

To finish we had the coyote incidence, which has been well documented already.

Then we rode into Santa Monica where Sandra and Bernice our ever-present support crew awaited us, along with friends and family. I finished and phoned my daughter my challenge complete.

The crew of Will, Kenny, Steve, Ian, James and tour leader Greg we thank you, we would in no way have completed this without you guys.

Mick, Andy, Dan, Bazza, Casey, Mark and Ross it was a pleasure to ride with you all, I know we all gave everything we had.

The lads are planning a tour of Europe in two years, put your name down places will be available because

I know I will never top what we achieved on Route 66, so I won't be involved. (Don't ask me when I've had a drink either.)

Cheers
Kevee

10/11/13
I met half of the team at a party last night and everyone looked a lot more refreshed than they did three weeks ago. Our challenge is nearly complete but not quite yet. Mick is currently checking through all the payments for Ball places and auction prizes, I believe most of the money is in now. We still have a couple of buckets at builder's merchants that we will pick up this week. You can still donate on the Virgin page if you would like, we would love you to and the charities certainly need you to.

I saw Steve's photos yesterday, about 700 in total and it took me back to my time on the road, we are hoping to load them all up on here at some point. We have got some interesting video footage coming so keep a look out for that.

Ross and Mick are busy planning the next adventure for 2016 and are keeping it under wraps at the moment as to what it is.

Andy is still missing Bag, but alas we hear he is on his way home.

Bal and Dan are back in training for a one day 200 mile challenge which looks terrific but lucky for me it's at the same time as my 25th wedding anniversary, so I have a get out of jail card.

Casey was back on the rugby field yesterday and looked to be enjoying himself. His mates Tommy and Sam look like they are up for a cycle challenge!!!

I have not seen Mark he has a busy diary, but we are hoping the whole team will be out next month for a social.

I have been cracking on with the book and hope to have it out early next year.

The more I delve back over the two years the more I think the challenge of getting to the start line was harder than the ride itself. Most of the guys have told me to write it how it was, it would be a boring book if it were all sweetness and light. So that's what you will be getting a true account of the trip.

Lastly, for all the people who have said they will buy the book when it comes out I thank you, it really is encouraging and is helping me on my way.

Cheers
Kevee

23/11/13

I have been a bit busy of late so sorry for not posting. The guys want me to keep going until all the money is in and sorted.

The Willow Foundation have invited us to a celebration day for fundraisers and we are certainly looking forward to that, how funny that of all the places it could be it is being held at The David Lloyd gym where Ross, Casey and myself carried out most of our training.

I have done no training whatsoever since I got back, I'm thinking 1 January as I did last year!!!

Since we returned so many people have congratulated us and I thank you all for your support, people who I hadn't seen for years had been following the blog and Twitter and knew all about the ups and downs of the trip.

The book is going well and should be complete by Christmas, so hopefully it will be out early next year.

You are part of a team for two years, constantly talking to each other, emails, Facebook and phone messages, it's kind of weird when it stops. We are all back at work and slipping back into a normal regime. Were having a reunion in a couple of weeks so I might get some news on who's up to what, its been very quiet from all of us perhaps we needed some time with our families.

I seem to be attending a lot of 50th birthday parties at the moment, lucky for me not mine yet, that's a long way off. I'm certainly out of practice drinking, my dancing seems ok (dad dancing) but I was very outclassed on my alcohol consumption.

Don't forget if you are looking for a charity challenge it's easier than you think, check out The Do it for Charity/Skyline Events websites they have hundreds of ideas, I'm giving them a plug because they looked after us on the trip and re-tweeted everything we put out whilst on the trip as did The Willow Foundation.

Thanks for that.

Sorry if the blog is a bit short and none too witty but I have been writing for seven hours today and my mind has gone a bit flat. Let's hope we don't have to listen to Wham, Duran Duran or *We Are The Bloody Champions* tonight at the 50th party and definitely not the song where all old people sit on the floor and think there in a boat, "What's that all about, God only knows."

Cheers
Kevee

8/12/13
The big Route 66 reunion is next Friday, all riders apart from Andy are attending.

Some of the crew are coming down from as far as Manchester (fair play Ian).

The beer will be flowing and the memories will come flooding back. I have all but forgotten the smell of the RV toilet and I'm hoping that memory doesn't come flooding back. Mick and Ross have been putting a European event together, I'm not allowed to give too many details and I don't know that many, but I have heard through the grapevine it will not be half as gruelling as Route 66, opting for Hotels rather than 24 hour riding. The event will take place 2016 I believe but don't quote me on that. I have also heard it will be a bigger group than Route 66. So places maybe up for grabs. I'm sure Mick and Ross will be making a big announcement in the not too distant future so keep checking back here. Mick is asking me to help crew it, as I don't want to partake this time, but I'm keeping my options open as to what I will be doing in two years' time. I did say I was hanging up my cycling shoes but my daughter has said she would like to cycle to Paris with me next August, having completed rides with Sandra and Casey I am very excited by the prospect of cycling with my daughter (Bex training starts 1 Jan). Dan and

Bazza are still cycling and training for the 200 mile in a day Majorca ride. Andy and Mick are still spinning (although judging by Mick's Facebook today it looks like the classes have moved from the gym to the pub) and I hear Andy is still losing weight!!!! Mark has a new bike on the way, but will he ride it or just stick it on a rack in the garage!!!! Ross is working hard on future challenge ideas. Casey is back playing rugby. I have agreed to play a game next week (why?)

The book is coming along I'm still looking to complete by Christmas, everyone wants to know what's in it? I keep telling everyone it is my take on the whole two years from start to finish, who was in, who left, raising the money, logistics, the ride itself, who rode what and when; but most of all it tells the tale of how much I enjoyed the whole experience and how I was feeling along the way. It may be witty it may not be witty I have had a laugh writing it, even the bits where stress and sleep deprivation were quite evident.

So the blogs will keep coming for a while longer, get ready for more events from Mick and Ross as they embark on their next round of fundraisers for the Europe challenge.

To all my L2P and Three Cities friends I hope to meet you on a cycle ride somewhere next year and to all my rugby friends please look after me on Saturday, I might be a bit fragile before the game after Friday night.

What was that blog all about? I don't really know

Cheers
Kevee

3/1/14

Another Year Another Blog

Happy New Year.

I know it's late but I have broken my finger in numerous places. I know what your thinking one of the other riders has decided that they don't want me to write the book and have somehow jinxed me, maybe they want the old, "What goes on tour stays on tour" scenario. Come on guys we had a great time including the dog attacks, the coyote incident, the torrential rain and the bloody wind. What about the Interstate where I'm sure some of the guys just shut their eyes and prayed for the exit. The odd row, the toilet (Jesus that was rough) getting lost and don't forget the potholes.

Friendships became strained but we all pulled through and can look back and think we did that together.

We have splintered off a bit since the trip and it was inevitable if you spend that much time together you probably need a bit of space after the event. My Facebook used to be jammed with messages as was my email. The constant phone calls day after day now it's oddly quiet.

So I start my New Year with these thoughts in my head,

1. Never play rugby again.
2. Finish the book.
3. Ride London to Paris one more time.
4. Try not to upset anyone (maybe this one will prove the most difficult!).
5. Attend the re-union drink in March and invite all our L2P and Three Cities friends along as it's been a while now.

I wish you all the best the blogs have just about run there course, we shall update you on future trips if any come off and I will update you on the book. As always thanks for your support without you lot reading the blog there would have been no point writing it.

Cheers
Kevee

Lightning Source UK Ltd.
Milton Keynes UK
UKOW03f0711090314

227799UK00001B/13/P